## THE AUTHOR

Frank Norman was born in Bristol on 9 June 1930. He was illegitimate. Handed over by his mother to a Church of England adoption society, he was sent out on trial to a succession of foster parents but they all handed him back. The last, an aristocratic lady in Kensington, delivered him to Dr Barnardo's Homes. He was then seven and did not leave the orphanage until 1946, when he was sixteen.

Barnardo's found him a job in a nursery garden, but he hated it and ran away with a travelling fair. He soon discovered London, and Soho in particular, where he worked in various spielers (illegal gambling dens), worked his apprenticeship as a burglar and discovered the charms of shopping with a stolen cheque book. He spent several short spells in prison culminating in three years 'corrective training'. The experience was so appalling that he decided to go straight and write a book about it, *Bang to Rights* (also published by The Hogarth Press). Stephen Spender published an excerpt first in *Encounter* in 1958 and Raymond Chandler wrote an introduction to it.

Although he had no grasp of grammar or spelling, Frank Norman did have a hilarious gift as a raconteur, and was quickly taken up by literary London. His first stage play, *Fings Ain't Wot They Used T'be*, written for Joan Littlewood's Theatre Workshop at Stratford East, was a smash hit and made him famous. He went on to become the author of thirteen books, several plays, television and film scripts and various articles. Frank Norman's marriage in 1971 to Geraldine Keen, a 'posh' journalist on *The Times*, outraged some, surprised everyone and proved an enormous success. He died of Hodgkin's Disease in 1980.

# BANANA BOY

Frank Norman

*New Introduction by
Richard Cobb*

THE HOGARTH PRESS
LONDON

Published in 1987 by
The Hogarth Press
Chatto and Windus Ltd
40 William IV Street, London WC2N 4DF

First published in Great Britain by Martin Secker and Warburg Ltd 1969
Copyright © Frank Norman 1969
Introduction copyright © Richard Cobb 1987

All rights reserved. No part of this publication may be reproduced, stored in a retrieval system, or transmitted in any form, or by any means, electronic, mechanical, photocopying, recording or otherwise, without the prior permission of the publisher.

British Library Cataloguing in Publication Data

Norman, Frank
Banana Boy – (Hogarth lives and letters)
1. Dr. Barnardo's   2. England – Social Life
and customs – 20th century
I. Title
362.7'32'0924    HV1146

ISBN 0 7012 0684 5

Printed in Great Britain by
Cox & Wyman Ltd
Reading, Berkshire

# INTRODUCTION

I only knew Frank Norman fairly late in his life when he was in his mid-forties, had married Geraldine Keen, and had established an international reputation as a populist writer, playwright and autobiographer. The first time we met was at the home of Geraldine's brother Maurice, a colleague of mine at Oxford, and Frank told me then that he had started to write thanks to the encouragement of Stephen Spender, who had published an account of his prison experiences, and had strongly urged him to write more. I met him on several occasions after that. At first I found him far from reassuring. There was a contained violence about him, something tigerish; he had an ugly scar on his face, his very stillness seemed menacing. On our second meeting, one of my children accidentally spilled some beer that he was drinking out of a pint mug, his dark eyes flashed with rage behind his glasses, and I thought for a moment that he was going to spring. But he reined in his sudden anger. Later, he got used to my wife and myself, no longer treating us with wary suspicion, but greeting us with a very communicative warmth. I suppose he felt the need to test people out at first. The last time we saw him was on a summer Sunday in a pretty house in a Gloucestershire village. We had driven over for lunch. I remember the peaceful setting and the tranquility of Frank. After lunch, we all went for a walk beside a field of long corn. He had by then come a long way. Above all, he had found happiness. The last ten years of his life were a compensation for the misery and the lack of love of his bleak institutional childhood and adolescence. Frank and Geraldine, although from totally different backgrounds – they could not have been more different – formed from the start a wonderfully matched couple, who yet managed to respect one another's separate areas of privacy.

Frank still had his weekly nights out on the town, doing the rounds of his old Soho haunts and looking in on his own old pals, while Geraldine got on with her job as Sales Correspondent of *The Times*. It was a measure of her affection and her perceptiveness that she at once spotted Frank's need for at least a residue of privacy, the loss of which he had suffered in his ten years of institutional existence in the Homes. The very success of their marriage seemed to fly in the face of the iron English laws of class. They also shared an anarchistic attitude to the outer world. I think what she, above all, gave to Frank was the certitude of being loved and the security of a home, of a base to which he could return from his nocturnal wanderings (he comments, wryly, of the war years, most of which he spent at Cardington Abbey, the Barnado's home in Bedford: '... the real horror of the war was never clear to me, I would never be told that a loved one of mine had been killed for I had no loved ones, my house could not be bombed for I did not have one ...'). Alas, their shared happiness was brought to a sudden, brutal end by Frank's last, terrible illness. He was only fifty when he died.

I admired Frank as a writer for his ironic humour (I was very flattered when, on one occasion, I managed to send him into fits of laughter at a most unedifying story I told him about myself and a fair-haired English girl I had met in a Paris cinema), his marvellously spontaneous verbal inventiveness, his cockney pluck (he was, in fact, a cockney by conversion, not by birth – he was born in Bristol), his readiness to laugh at himself, and his descriptive imagination. He was a very *visual* writer, picking out the red and white dots of a girl's summer dress (with nothing on underneath it, he adds, being engagingly explicit about these things, in another book); the battered bowler and the three days' growth of beard of a fairground operator; the awful shock at the revelation, back in the cruel light of day, of the ugliness of a girl encountered in the comforting warm and perfumed blackness of a big cinema at Waltham Cross, a girl with codlike eyes. In a similar vein, he describes his first sexual experience, 'with a fat girl guide inside a smelly disused pillbox up against the wall ...' He refers to his two visits to a tattoo artist in Dalston. On the first visit he has tattooed on his right forearm 'a rather nationalistic looking lady carrying a sword (supposedly to protect her honour) and wearing high boots, a flowing cape and trapeze-artist leotard. The whole thing was done in blue and red indelible ink . . .' The next time he opts for a naval motif: 'an anchor, incorporating anchor-chain, sailor's head and distant sunset . . .'

He has the knack, too, of bringing out the dreary, yet semi-comical, banality of trolley-bus-terminal topography on the northern edges of London – Enfield, Dalston, Ponders End, and the ever-persistent Waltham Cross ('On Saturday afternoons the local talent, both boys and girls, congregated outside Woolworth's in Waltham Cross High Street') – the dim, seedy borderlands between the vast city and that indefinable county: Herts. Some of the worst years of his childhood had been in Bedford, followed, briefly, by Kingston-on-Thames, then Herts; and his suburbia is funny, totally unassuming, pathetic, and rather sad.

Having led, a few months on from the trolley-bus-terminal circuit, a picaresque existence as a writer, Frank Norman is especially well qualified to invite us to take to the freedom of the open road, to the soothing darkness of the rural night which, even as a child, holds no fears for him. Even the hoots of owls bring the promise of escape and freedom. In *Banana Boy*, there are two quite breathless accounts of running away. Of course, on both occasions it all ends up pretty badly, despite the unexpected kindness displayed by a Bedfordshire farmer's wife and by a rural bobby; the boy is caught, brought back to face the music. But, at the end of the book, we watch him, just turned sixteen, on the eve of getting clean away: 'I had enrolled in the university of life.' No wonder, from the time of his stay in the dreadful Bedford Home (where the dark Hilda May gave him nits), he felt an affinity with the gypsies. While in the Homes (so unlike the pretty rural cottages of the Barnardo's collecting boxes to be seen in pubs and clubs during the thirties, forties and fifties), he had often thought of running away to sea. But he never got beyond having that naval tattoo on his left forearm.

Frank Norman is not only a very visual writer, especially when describing the anonymous wasteland on the northern rim of London, he also knows how to use his ears, which are well attuned to the vagaries of cockney speech. The bowler-hatted fairground operator is prepared to take him on, provided he can produce a work-book and can assure him that he has not done time (that would come later and would be the subject of another book). ' "I'll take ya word for it, fahsands wouldn't," he laughed, "all I'm short of is bovva wiv the law . . ." ' And his workmate tells him: ' "You start that side an' I'll start the uvva . . ." '

The every-watchful, quick-footed, wry humour helps him through the years of rejection and the absence of love in the dreadful Homes, ten years during which he is denied not only tenderness, but even the tiny luxury of a Christian name: just Norman. But before this, between the ages of four and seven, he is the object of several tentative efforts to get him adopted on the part of the sinister-sounding Church of England Adoption Society. And he seems indeed to have been adopted two or three times, once by a lady in Southsea. But it has not worked; he is always sent back; a bit like a parcel, Returned to Sender. Then comes the awful moment of betrayal when, at the age of seven, he is abandoned by Lady W. and brought by the smiling Uncle D. (the cruelty of that 'uncle'!) to the headquarters in London. 'So that was it,' he comments, 'the final abandonment, being signed away like lost property.' And thence to Cardington Abbey, Bedford. 'I was well aware that the Bedford Home [which had dormitories with awful, hearty names like *Peekaboo*] was for 'backward' children and in protest I would on occasions run about the lawn outside Miss Duke's window [Miss Duke was the grim, unsmiling Scottish Headmistress] – backwards.' In 1943, he reached the age of thirteen. 'By the time I was thirteen I had become a strapping great lad with an expression on my face that looked as though it should have been on a police WANTED photograph.' (Frank is, of course, always prone to turn his sharp, biting humour against himself, no doubt as an essential part of his survival kit designed and improved upon to get him through the wretched, heartless institutional years. The book has, on the back of the Dedication to his daughter, Sally Norman, the following quote: 'Ernest Hemingway was once asked: "What is the best early training for a writer?" He replied: "An unhappy childhood." ') No doubt his description of himself is accurate enough. Certainly, three years later, when he is sixteen, and about to leave the last of the Homes, the 'Situation Photograph', which he includes in the book, evidently with a purpose, makes him look rather alarming: the large, dark eyes seem to shine with hate (he observes elsewhere that this was his dominant sentiment throughout the ten years), and the thick watery lips are not reassuring.

By this time, Frank is at Goldings, a Home in Hertfordshire. As a result, he will go through life as an Old Goldolian – an expression he applies to himself derisively as another example of that jolly vocabulary favoured by Barnardo's, no doubt in conscious and rather ghastly imitation of a public school (not, it is true, an entirely dissimilar institution, at least in respect of rotten food, lack of privacy and organised brutality). Much to Frank's amazement, he discovers, once he has achieved a measure of fame in the sixties, that the headquarters in London like to keep up with the fortunes – or the misfortunes – of its old boys and old girls. One wonders if there is not an O.G. tie; it seems in character. Anyhow, Goldings is even worse than Cardington Abbey, Bedford. 'You had to be tough, or you went under. Indeed one boy died whilst I was there; it was said to have been from natural causes, but then some causes are more natural than others . . .' In a lighter vein, he writes of the same Home: 'the cockroaches in the kitchen outnumbered the boys ten to one. During the day they hid behind the steam coppers, but at night they ventured forth for a little exercise . . .' At Goldings, he makes a friend of Ginger, 'the coarsest boy I had ever met, he was always playing with himself and masturbated nightly after lights out . . . "Ninety-nine change hands," he would laugh when he came into the kitchen after a hard night's jerking-off . . . indeed I am certain that he could have wanked for Britain in the Olympics and won the gold medal with ease . . .' Such were the austere extra-curricular activities of Goldings. Frank, too – and he is always baldly explicit on the subject of his own sexual activities and those of his companions-in-misery – seems to have got his hand in there.

His most ferocious humour, however, is reserved for the menacing presence of a dominant and singularly unloving religion as a prop to the rigours of a grinding discipline and general deprivation, both physical and moral: ten years without a Christian name – never once: Frank – but ten years of a formal Christianity of the muscular, Anglican variety, as an accompaniment to such manly activities as boxing or singing 'Under the Spreading Chestnut Tree' (a song for which Frank retains a hearty loathing years afterwards). The Church Established and Barnardo's march in step. Poor Frank, ever since the age of four (the Church of England Adoption Society), has churchy people being nosily solicitous about his moral welfare. The local clergy emerge as the active partners of a heartless system. 'In the afternoon we went to Sunday School where we sang: "Jesus wants me for a sunbeam" and were read religious allegories with stings in their tails . . . ' At Christmas, the presents (from charitable organisations) 'were dished out by the local vicar dressed up in a Father Christmas outfit; it was the only time in my life that I have seen Santa wearing a dog-collar . . .' In one of the Homes, the boy, in a pathetic effort to capture something of the Christmas spirit, makes a pretty calendar, with holly and snow and robins, which he places surreptitiously on the desk of a master whom he quite likes. The master, on finding the calendar the next morning, suspects his motives and tells him off. The timid gesture has been a complete failure, Frank ponders sorrowfully 'as we marched down the hill to church . . .' This is not the only time in the book that Frank reveals, beneath all his bluster and biting humour, beneath his outer casing of toughnesss, an underlying sympathy that is striving desperately to get out, and a quite Dickensian sentimentality; here in an attempt – futile, of course – to escape from the military style, church-parade rigours of a regimented Christmas.

There is, too, a joyfully irreverent description of confirmation: 'The Bishop [of Bedford] sat on a throne . . . and blessed each child as they stepped forward and knelt before him. The whole thing was somewhat reminiscent of a conveyor-belt, as one after the other they received the "laying on of hands" and a mumbled prayer . . .'; training, of a sort, however, for Frank's subsequent employment in a tin-box factory in Enfield as a Perforator of Talcum Powder Tops Hand Press Operator: 'Christian name (put the top on the press); surname (pull the handle, let it go and dispose of finished product)' – all to the accompaniment of the magical words: 'Loretta Young'. Frank's final word on the subject comes a little later: 'During the whole of my childhood God the Father, God the Son and God the Holy Ghost were rammed down my throat, like over-sold pop stars . . .' It has been a brand of religion that could certainly not ever have been described as one of Love.

Frank was admitted to his first Home in March 1937, at the aged of seven. He was finally released from Barnardo's not very tender care in October 1946. Much of his time spent in these establishments coincided with the war years. But the war made very little impact on the lives of the inmates, and one of the singular insights provided by this remarkable book – so ferocious, and yet so tender – is the way in which the private and the public calenders run side by side, without ever joining. The book comes as an assertion of the primacy of private over public history, a historical theme that I have always found vaguely consoling as a defence against totalitarianism. In this respect, the totalitarianism is within the Home, not outside it. Still, it is comforting thus to have illustrated, in the uncertain chronicle of childhood memory, the *irrelevance* of war.

Cardington Abbey, it is true, is next to an important airfield; in 1939, the boys cannot fail to notice the bustle of activity next door. There is a big map of the Continent pinned up in one of the classrooms. 'On days when I was feeling particularly badly treated, I wished that the Germans would hurry, for I felt sure that they would release me from my torment . . .' But none come and no enemy aircraft ever gets as far up as Bedford. 1940 is recalled only as a bitterly cold winter in the course of which the Ouse bursts it banks. As by then there is much less activity at the airfield, 'quite naturally I took it for granted that the war was now over, though I had not the slightest idea who had won it . . .' 'Our schooling continued uninterrupted by the global holocaust . . . There was also a good deal of hiding behind trees, walls, and: "Bang bang! You're dead!" ' All the time the *real* calendar is a strictly internal one, in both senses, and one that allows no space for outside events but plenty in the tummy: Monday: mince; Tuesday: Toad in the Hole; Wednesday: bacon; Thursday: tripe (ugh! – poor Frank lives in dread of Thursdays); Friday: fish; Saturday: Shepherd's Pie; Sunday: roast meat (so there is something to be said for Sunday after all).

In August 1941, he is transferred to Kingston, where the war is a bit nearer. Soon after his transfer, six Spanish boys, orphans from the Republican side of the Civil War, turn up at the Home. One of them is the delightful Pedro, who becomes Frank's best friend. Never, the boys are told, pick up objects – fountain pens, powder puffs, combs – scattered in the street: they might be German booby-traps. Frank finds a use for his empty gas-mask container, as a vehicle for *Craven A*, and other products of the black market. In 1943, a boy loses his right forefinger in a bread-slicing machine. Frank reflects that the incident may turn out to be quite a lucky accident: it would get him out of military service some time in the future (a characteristic display of his wonderfully anarchic wisdom, acquired in the hard school of enforced 'togetherness'; how we can appreciate that Frank will never, ever be a Joiner!). The reality is not the war, as it rumbles away in the distance, but 'the smell of boys . . . the cruel staff . . . the complete lack of privacy . . .' In 1945, 'the war was over. There was much jubilation but it didn't seem to affect us overmuch . . .' In the summer of that year, it is true, the boys do get a trip to the seaside (St Mary's Bay, in Kent, where Frank gets his sexual experience with the fat girl guide: another example of putting public events, in this case Victory, to good private use). And that is that.

What more is there to say about this sad, wry, wise,

humorous yet tender book? The best thing is to read it – and to enjoy every line of it.

*Richard Cobb, Wolvercote 1986*

# *Contents*

| | |
|---|---|
| Introduction | 1 |
| Earliest Remembrances | 7 |
| Bedford | 17 |
| Kingston | 51 |
| Goldings | 104 |
| My Situation | 135 |

# *List of Illustrations*

| | |
|---|---|
| At Cardington Abbey *facing page* | 6 |
| Kingston boys | 7 |
| Goldings | 38 |
| The 'Situation Photograph' | 39 |

FOR MY DAUGHTER
SALLY NORMAN

Ernest Hemingway was once asked: 'What is the best early training for a writer?' He replied: 'An unhappy childhood.'

# *Introduction*

APART FROM THE OMISSION of several names, this is the first page of my Dr Barnardo's dossier.

### *PRIVATE & CONFIDENTIAL*

JOHN FRANK NORMAN. (*Illegitimate*) *Admitted 24.3.1937.*
BORN: *9.6.1930 at 155 Whiteladies Road, Bristol.*
BAPTIZED: *C. of E. No particulars. Mother C. of E.*
LAST SIX MONTHS ADDRESS: *c/o Mrs A., Prittlewell, Southend-on-Sea.*
LAST SCHOOL ATTENDED: *Barnes Private School, Church Road, Barnes.*
PAYMENT: PERIOD: AGREEMENT: INFORMATION
*See below.* *Six months* *None.* FROM:
*probation.* *Report (Kim)*
APPLICANT: *Lady W., 45 Onslow Square, South Kensington, London, S.W.7.*
MOTHER: *Beatrice Spence Smith née Norman (30); health was good; character indifferent, separated from her husband; last known address – 1 Hudds Vale, St George's, Bristol.*
FATHER: (*Putative*): *Frank Charles Booth (35); Engineer;*

£800 per annum; M.; 'Netherleigh', Highfield, Llandaff, Cardiff, Wales. Not affiliated.

MOTHER'S HUSBAND: *Vernon Leslie Smith; married the mother 23.1.31. at Bristol Register Office; no other particulars.*

HALF-BROTHER OR SISTER: *Child of the mother's marriage, no other particulars.*

*The mother is described as an adventuress. At the time she met the putative father, she was a secretary at some works. She married in 1931, and her present address is unknown. When last heard of, two years ago, she was separated from her husband, and the child of the marriage was boarded out.*

*The putative father is the son of a managing director of an Engineering Works, and is very well off financially. After John was born, the putative father paid the mother through a solicitor the sum of £300 in order to clear his name. Later the mother made herself a nuisance, and in June 1933, Mr Buttle, of the Church of England Adoption Society, was asked by the putative father's mother to get John adopted. For a short time the putative father paid £1 per week, while John was in the Society's Home at Kingsbury. John was sent to several people, with a view to adoption, but each time he was returned with such excuses as being untruthful, dishonest and unintelligent.*

*Two years ago, applicant, who is Roman Catholic, made herself responsible, through the Adoption Society, for the maintenance of John, but did not legally adopt him. He was boarded out by applicant with Mrs A., at Prittlewell, Southend, for about eighteen months prior to last September. He was then brought to London and handed over to the care of a Mr and Mrs M., White Hart Lane, Barnes, who contemplated adopting him. On 12.2.1937 Mr M., took him back to applicant, as not being suitable. He has remained in her care ever since. Applicant states that she cannot afford to keep him, and there are reasons why she cannot keep him, but she wishes to keep in touch with him. When our officer called, the conditions in applicants home were not at all good, and it was reported that John should not be allowed to remain there a day longer than necessary.*

*John is a weak-looking child, and mentally backward, but he has never had a chance, being pushed about from pillar to post. At school he was said to be quite docile and friendly. The putative father should be persuaded to contribute regularly towards John's maintenance.*
F.M.A.

This extraordinary document came into my possession during 1966, Doctor Barnardo's centenary year. I had seen several religious television programmes where the praises of Barnardo's Homes were sung and several saintly articles in the Press about the great man himself: there came not a word of dissent from any quarter. I was astonished and rather angered at all this abject veneration, for I spent almost ten years in one and another of their Homes and enjoyed hardly a minute of it. Far from being in Elysium, I remember above all being unloved and cruelly treated. The great barns in which I was housed together with several hundred other orphans at Bedford, Kingston upon Thames and Hertford were all more reminiscent of Dotheboys Hall than the delightfully pretty cottage collection boxes that I have seen in pubs and clubs all over the country.

I resolved to write an article about my life and times in the institutions and be damned. I wrote immediately to the head office at Stepney Causeway, London, E.1, and requested the General Superintendent's co-operation in letting me have some information about myself before I was admitted to the Homes and perhaps some details from their file on me. To my utter amazement they told me everything I needed to know and indeed sent me a detailed account of my progress (perhaps it would be better to say lack of progress) in the Homes. They also agreed to let me have (at my request) the first page of my dossier. Could the austere organization have gone soft or were they afraid of what I might write if they did not co-operate? I doubt if the latter is true; about the former I cannot say, nor does it concern me here.

It is against Barnardo's policy to give old girls and boys documented information about themselves, though they are not opposed to telling them anything they want to know verbally. In my case obviously an exception was made, perhaps because they were persuaded of my serious intent.

I took a representative of theirs to an expensive lunch and from his briefcase (over coffee) he produced the faded pink (and no doubt much-read) folder, which he opened on the table in front of us. I was amused to find that a good deal of its contents consisted of reviews of my early books and plays, articles I had written and features that had appeared about me in the national Press years ago, by such people as Nancy Spain and Gilbert Harding. So they are still keeping a record of my activities, I thought. There seemed to be no recent publicity, but then I might easily have missed seeing it, for whilst I was permitted to look, the look was brief.

It was after this lunch that it was agreed at head office to give me every assistance. Several days later a fat envelope arrived in the post containing a mass of factual data. Much of this I was well aware of, but just as much was a complete revelation to me, particularly that first page. I had no idea where I had come from prior to being admitted to the Homes, though I knew that I had been born in Bristol. I had discovered this at the age of about seventeen or eighteen when I had to produce my birth certificate for some reason or other. I obtained the document from Somerset House and was horrified to discover that I was not a Cockney sparrow after all. Since my release from Barnardo's I had convinced myself and everyone else that I was born within the sound of Bow Bells. I developed, in an uncontrived sort of way, a fantastically broad Cockney accent and even invented a family and my place of birth – Christian Street, off the Commercial Road, E.1. I told everyone that my father was a costermonger down Roman Road market. When pressed by anyone for further information I simply said that I was a bastard and had been brought up mainly in institutions, but never said which one. Through keeping up the pretence I was accepted as one of 'our own' by Cockneys at large and the criminal fraternity in particular. It is difficult to say why I kept up the deception for so many years, though I imagine that the short answer is simply that I needed to belong somewhere, and it is easier, if you have no references, to be accepted by the lower orders than by the middle or upper classes.

When at the age of twenty-six I turned my hand and mind to writing it seemed the most natural thing in the world to me to write about the Cockney labyrinth that I knew so well, and by omission still keep concealed the real truth of my early years – which were in any event in large part a mystery to me. As a result my public *persona* is that of the 'scar-faced, ex-jailbird, illegitimate son of a costermonger.' What better image for the author of *Fings Ain't Wot They Used T'be?*

I make this explanation mainly for the benefit of those who have read my other autobiographical books. I have rarely if ever been less than truthful about my past life, in print. It is simply that I had not written about my childhood until an article of mine appeared in the March 1967 issue of *Encounter*, bearing the same title as this book.

Though on the records my first name is John, I do not remember being called by it since my very early childhood, perhaps up to the age of five, certainly no later than seven.

It is interesting to note that I have my father's Christian name, putative though he may have been, and my mother's maiden name – *filius nullius* truly a bastard am I. If my mother had married Mr Booth my name would very likely have been John Booth, or, conversely, if I had gone to live with the man that she did marry, JOHN SMITH! As it is I have been put in this world to begin my own dynasty; as yet I have not been able to produce a son, but there is still time perhaps.

From studying Debrett's Peerage I discover that Lady W., (from whom no doubt I get my arrogance) died several years ago. Nevertheless I feel that it would be unfair of me to say who she was, from natural good taste and fear of embarrassing the eminent members of her illustrious family. As to the other names that I have omitted from the dossier, I remember none of them clearly and imagine that they only laid hands on me through answering ads in the personal columns of *The Times* – 'Nanny wanted for five-year-old boy' – or some such.

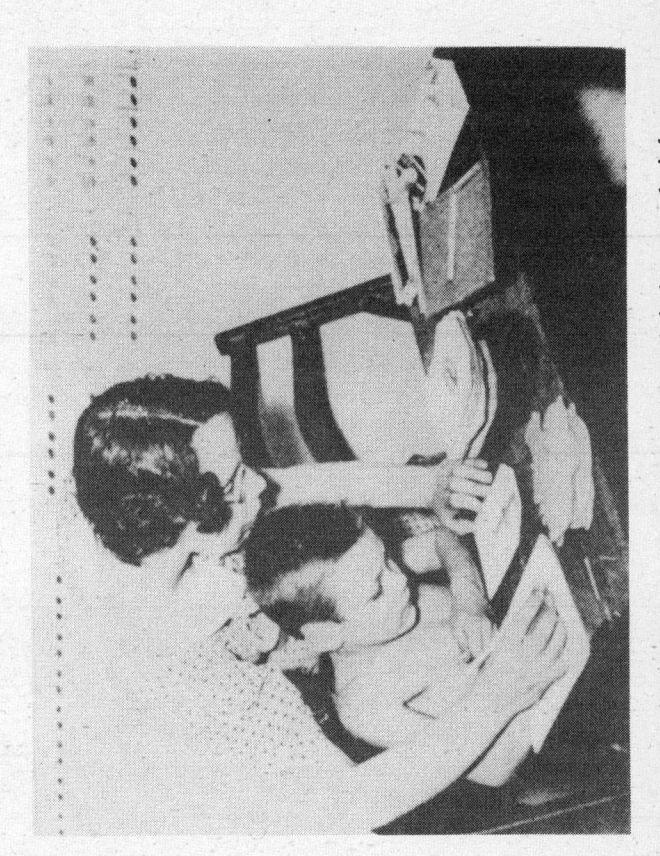

At Cardington Abbey learning the alphabet, aged eight

Kingston boys. It is likely that the author is one of them!

# Earliest Remembrances

A LINE IN THE DOSSIER which has caused me considerable puzzlement reads '. . . conditions in applicant's home were not at all good.' It was an observation of the Barnardo's officer who called at the house in Onslow Square. I cannot for the life of me imagine what he meant. For I remember vividly that life with Lady W. was sumptuous and graceful; there were servants and maids, below stairs in the kitchen there was a chef, there was over the whole household a great atmosphere of opulence. Liveried delivery men brought groceries, fish, meat and vegetables to the tradesman's entrance in the basement, from Fortnum's and Harrods no doubt, though I cannot truly swear to it. I can remember that Lady W. was an eccentric, and there always seemed to be a lot of bottles about. Was this what the worthy children's officer had been referring to? It could be, but if so it seems rather hard. But then Barnardo's are renowned for their piety, indeed never in my life have I come across such a devout lot of Christians as the masters and mistresses in whose charge I found myself from 1937 to 1946. Their speciality was the rod and the good book. They chastised us unmercifully, the Bible in one hand and a cane in the other.

Looking into the kaleidoscope of my childhood memories,

the house in Onslow Square is the most vivid. A mental picture of it has imprinted itself in my mind, and I am certain that if I ever visited it again I would know my way around as though I had left it only yesterday instead of thirty years ago. The extraordinary thing is that, until I saw the address in the dossier I had never been able to work out exactly where it was. For many years I had thought that it was in the country – because of the trees and shrubs in the square opposite I expect. To a small child it must have looked like acres of farmland. There was also Hyde Park just up the road, where I remember being taken almost daily; in those days sheep grazed there in the Spring. But I also remember there being railings outside the house; I have never seen country houses with railings outside them. Then there were the buses and lots of traffic about. Upon reflection it could have only been London or some other big city, it was simply the greenery that led me to believe otherwise.

Lady W. had a TV set, which was indeed a rare thing in those days. I saw King George V's funeral on it, and was enthralled by the spectacle of the bier, bearing the King's coffin draped with the Union Jack; it was drawn along the streets by a detachment of sailors, escorted by sombre horse guards, riding shiny jet-black steeds. Naturally, I thought the whole ritual was going on in the magic box, acted out by Lilliputians. But I was sad that George V had died, he was the Sailor King and my idol. In my early teens I longed to run away to sea, and even went to the extent of having an anchor tattooed on my left forearm, which was the nearest I ever came to doing it.

For some reason that I have never been able to define I was never allowed upstairs during the day. My nursery was at the back of the house on the ground floor and for the most part I was confined to that room, though I was also allowed into the dining-room, in which there was a piano and a huge dining-table around which I used to run pell mell until puffed out. I was also permitted to play on the pavement outside the house; I used to chi-ike the tradesmen mercilessly as they arrived with deliveries for the house. Once I so enraged the chef that he chased me all over the house with a carving knife – it was all in fun I am sure, but I was terrified and screamed my head off. I also told on him at the earliest opportunity. I do not know if he was reprimanded, but he never chased me again.

In the evenings Lady W. would summon me to her sitting room on the first floor. I was never hard to find, for I always sat on the stairs waiting for her call, and would scamper up as fast as my legs would carry me. Lady W. was, I remember, an ample woman, in her early forties I should think; she had a nice face and warm affectionate brown eyes. I knew that she liked me a lot, but she never mollycoddled me. She treated me rather as though I was a little grown-up – in the manner of emancipated women. She would stroke my head and pat my cheek affectionately, then, indicating that I should sit at her feet, she would settle her ample frame into a huge armchair and read to me from *Tom Brown's Schooldays*, *Beyond the Blue Mountain* and children's stories. I remember one story in particular about a tiger who chased a little boy around a tree so fast that he turned into butter – the tiger, that is. The predominant colour in the room was brown, the carpet, curtains and furniture were all brown; it was a rich brown like polished oak, warm and comforting like hot chocolate.

'Frank, dear, I think it is time you went off to bed,' she would say all too soon. It was she, I am certain, who changed my name from John to Frank, that is to say used my second name instead of my first. I loved that room and looked forward to being invited into it by my benefactor more than anything else in the world.

Now and then Aunty Mary and Uncle D. used to come to the house to see us. Uncle D. was Lady W.'s brother (I discovered from Debrett) and Aunty Mary was his wife, I think. He was very tall and aristocratic-looking, his black hair shiny and sleeked back very close to his head. Aunty Mary gushed and kissed me a lot, which I absolutely loathed; I well remember squirming about like an eel in her arms, wildly trying to make my escape. Uncle D. frightened me a little, mainly I think because of his great height; he also smelt of tobacco. One day they brought me a present of a china doll, I put it on a chair and later sat on the chair, completely forgetting that I had left the doll on it. There was a muffled crunch like a cup being broken under bed-clothes, and a large piece of the now fragmented china slashed open the inside of my left thigh. Blood spurted in all directions, drenching the chair and my clothes. Aunty Mary let out a great shriek, I went very pale I think, but certainly did not cry, at least not straight away. The doctor was sent for and several stitches were put in my thigh: I carry a thin white scar from the wound to this day.

It is rather surprising that I remember so many little anecdotes in connection with Lady W. and the house in Onslow Square, and hardly anything worth mentioning to do with the various people with whom I was boarded out. I can recollect being taken to the Kursaal at Southend-on-Sea. but not one thing about the lady who took care of me there, except that she used to bath me in the kitchen sink and that she wore a rubber apron whilst doing it. I remember having several mechanical toys, cars, trains and the like; I once caught my finger in the mainspring of one of them, it gripped onto it like a tenacious terrier, the more I tried to free myself the tighter the tortuous coil seemed to become. Though no doubt I was in great pain, my reaction was to fly into a blind rage, I roared about shouting and screaming at the top of my voice until someone eventually released me. The wound was only superficial and left no scar, for a change.

Occasionally Uncle D. would take me out on excursions to the Victoria and Albert Museum or Hyde Park. He walked very erect with his coat around his shoulders like Diaghilev; he also carried a cane with a silver knob on the end. I wonder if I wore a little Lord Fauntleroy suit – I can't remember, though I was certainly no urchin. He would stride along in his seven-league boots with me tearing along beside him, trying desperately to keep up. For that I certainly had to do, he never paused to wait for me if I lagged behind. If I did not keep abreast of him I would simply be left behind and there was an end to it. In the V. & A. I would race up and down the galleries looking first at one antiquity and then another, wishing to see absolutely everything but observing nothing. In the Park we would pause to look at the ducks, but I never had any bread to feed them, I expect Lady W. thought that far beneath my dignity.

I dimly recall being taken to the cinema in the West End one day. The main feature was a jungle film and I screamed the place down for I thought that the reptiles and wild animals were coming out of the screen after me. For some time after that I had a recurring nightmare about wild beasts tearing me limb from limb and gobbling me up; I would wake in the middle of the night screaming with terror. To allay my fears Lady W. bought me a nightlight which I kept on my bedside table. The lamp was a tiny replica of a village Church, inside which was a candle; when lit the warm light shone through the stained-glass windows, giving off an aura of comfort and protection. Through some baffling trick of physics the Church would rotate on a spindle when the candle was alight; the light shining through the stained-glass windows would then cast eerie shadows on the walls which frightened me as much as the nightmares. I was also petrified of the shadows cast across the ceiling by the branches of the trees in the square opposite the house. They looked to me like great clutching arms come to carry me off.

Under the wing of my benefactor the scene was set for a tale with uncanny echoes of *Great Expectations* with Lady W. playing Miss Havirsham and me playing Master Pip – I might have grown up to be one of those insufferable young men, Eton educated, with more money than sense and a pound-note accent like a Life Guards subaltern. But the rich tapestry of life being what it is, fate was soon to deal me an evil blow from which I was destined never to recover.

I cannot remember the exact moment when I sensed that all was not well at Onslow Square, I simply became aware of a subtle rejection. I do not remember behaving badly or being a nuisance, but knew that my presence in the house was responsible for the strange atmosphere that now prevailed. I seemed suddenly to see less of Lady W. and more of Aunty Mary and Uncle D., and there was much coming and going and whispers that I did not understand; had the novelty of having me around the place worn off? Had she tired of her pet? I cannot say, all I remember is that I was suddenly loved no more. During my last days at the tall white terraced house I was left almost entirely to my own devices; I sat alone at the dining-room window day after day watching pedestrians pass by. I knew that something dreadful was about to happen – I was going to be sent away. It was like waiting in the condemned cell for the day of execution. On the afternoon before my departure, I sat moodily on the window seat, when suddenly the butler entered the room carrying a huge cut-glass crystal cake-stand laden with every imaginable variety of sick-making cake – there were cream slices, apple puffs, strawberry flans, chocolate éclairs and gâteaux. My eyes lit up and grew larger than my stomach as he set the luxurious feast down on the table.

'They are all for you Master Frank,' said the dark-coated gentleman, discreetly retreating towards the door – I vividly remember that he always addressed me as Master Frank. When he had departed I stood for a time gazing at the wondrous sight. In my early childhood I was once read a fairy tale, the title of which now escapes me; it was about two young children lost in a dark forest. As they roamed about looking for a way out they came upon a cottage made of sweets and candy; I seem to remember that it was a salutary tale, its moral had to do with the evils of greed – it might have been *Hansel and Gretel*. Whenever I think of this story I think of my deliciously laden crystal cake-stand. I suppose I remember it so well because it was to be many years before I savoured such luxuries again.

Having gloated long enough, I took a cake from the stand and wolfed it down, then another and another – soon I was full but determined to finish the lot. Perhaps thinking that it would give me an appetite I began to run around the vast dining-room table, snatching a cake from the stand each time I passed it and eating it as I ran – I set myself the task of finishing the cake that I had taken by the time I had completed a circuit of the table. Within a short period of time I had crammed every last one inside me, leaving only the fancy paper doily upon the glistening stand and I am certain that I would have consumed that too had it been edible. In spite of my voracity I cannot recall feeling the slightest bit sick.

The following morning I was awakened early by the sound of subdued activity in the passage outside the nursery door. Though I did not know it immediately, the household were preparing for my departure from the house forever. Aunty Mary came into my room and got me up; I thought this odd for it was the first time I had seen her so early in the morning – I was usually washed and dressed by one of the servants.

As usual she fussed a lot, and told me that we were going out, but I sensed that there was more to it than that. Some nameless calamity awaited me that day, of that I was sure but in what guise I did not know. Within an hour or two I was to find out. Having dressed I was told to sit in the dining-room to await the arrival of Uncle D. who was to accompany us on our journey. As I passed along the passage to the dining-room I saw a small suit-case by the front door and knew that it contained my few belongings. As I sat forlorn on the edge of one of the high-backed dining-room chairs, Uncle D. entered the room with a cheerful smile on his face. I began to snivel for now I knew that something was dreadfully wrong, for whilst Uncle D. was not a miserable person he almost never smiled, except I think through embarrassment or nerves.

'The taxi will be here soon,' he said and then left me alone once more. Where on earth was Lady W? She was fantastically conspicuous by her absence; I expect she was upstairs too petrified to come down and say good-bye to me. Soon the taxi arrived and I was taken from the house screaming my head off – was Lady W. upstairs peering at me through the lace curtains as Aunty Mary and Uncle D. led me to the waiting taxi? Were her eyes like mine blinded with tears, her ample frame trembling with emotion? Perhaps it is just a romantic idea. The taxi rumbled off down the street and that was the last I saw of 45 Onslow Square nor did I hear a single word from Lady W, despite the note in my dossier about her wishing to keep in touch with me.

On weekdays I drink Bell's whisky but on alternate Saturdays I drink gin and vodka. On Sundays as a rule I drink nothing. On the Saturdays that I drink gin I get extremely maudlin and am rather inclined to end the day in tears. On one such Saturday not long ago, as drunk as the Lord I never became, I revisited Onslow Square in search of the house that I remember so well. It was two in the morning, and I had just left the house of a friend in the area – but for that I would not have bothered to make the pilgrimage. As I drunkenly wove my way along Sumner Place in the direction of Old Brompton Road I came to the square and read on the street sign that the odd numbers were on the other side. I continued to the opposite side as instructed and read 'Onslow Square numbers 41 to 75'. Thank goodness I have not got to walk the full length of the square, I thought, bracing my shoulders and breathing several lungfuls of the cold night air in an attempt to shake off some of the effects of the drink. By chance the night in question happened to be New Year's Eve and as I began to count the numbers I resolved that if Lady W.'s name (or that of any of her descendants) happened to be on the door I would ring the bell and reveal my identity to whoever answered the door. . . . 41, 43, 47, 49, 51, I'm pissed, I thought, and went back to the beginning again. 41, 43, 47, 49, 51. . . . How on earth can this be, where the hell is 45? It can't have simply vanished off the face of the poxy earth. I tried once more, carefully and methodically, but still the elusive number remained lost; for some time I stood gazing at the wall between 43 and 47 hoping ridiculously that the missing building would suddenly magically materialize before my very eyes. But nothing happened. I was suddenly seized with emotion and burst into floods of tears – reminiscent of the last time I had stood on that piece of pavement 30 years before. I rushed away and shall never return again to continue the black comedy.

I wonder if the taxi-driver knew what a fateful journey he was taking his young passenger on that spiritless March morning in 1937. I suppose not, but certainly he must have known that something was amiss from the aura of sadness that was upon us as he drew up outside Dr Barnardo's 'Ever-Open Door' at Stepney Causeway, E.1.

Aunty Mary took me by the hand and led me into the building. I was terrified and began to scream as loudly as my lungs would allow – it was as though I instinctively knew of the aggravation that was in store for me. Aunty Mary clasped me tightly to her bosom and tried to pacify me, but I would have none of it. I broke away from her and ran to a corner at the far end of the huge reception hall, bawling my head off – my screams ring in my ears even today. To one side of the hall there was a hatchway rather like a ticket office at a railway station. Uncle D. stood talking to someone on the other side of it, I did not hear what they were talking about but seem to remember some documents being signed. So that was it, the final abandonment, being signed away like lost property. I do not remember the exact moment that Aunty Mary and Uncle D. left, indeed I do not recall a single incident of the following ten days, during which time I was given various tests and a thorough medical examination. An extract from the doctor's report dated the same day as admission reads:

HEIGHT: *45½ inches*. WEIGHT: *48¾ lbs*. MEASLES: *No*. SCARLET FEVER: *No*. DIPHTHERIA: *No*. WHOOPING COUGH: *Yes*. TEETH: *F/G*. GENERAL PHYSIQUE: *F/G. Lymphatic Gland*. MENTAL CONDITION: *Backward (does not know letters)*. DISPOSITION: *?* GRADE: *B2*.

What a heart-melting, tear-jerking waif I must have been, but no tears were shed except my own.

# *Bedford*

ON 3 APRIL 1937 I was transferred from Barnardo's headquarters in Stepney to their home for 'backward' children at Bedford, which had the rather austere name of Cardington Abbey. I was accompanied on the journey by a frightening-looking matron, dressed from head to toe in black. I remember nothing of the journey except boarding the train; at our destination we were met by another matron dressed from head to toe in black. The second one took over responsibility for my delivery to the Home; the first took the next train back to London.

My first impression of Cardington Abbey was a mixture of awe, curiosity and fear. What manner of place was this that I had been brought to against my will, and why? The reception hall was vast. As I came through the solid oak front door, I was faced with a huge awe-inspiring stained-glass window depicting Jesus and several apostles. The floor was tiled and highly polished, there was a strong smell of fresh floor-polish. A great oak staircase led up to a gallery, off which were several rooms which served as the children's dormitories. Several idiot-looking children appeared in the gallery and peered down at me over the banister rail. There were both girls and boys, for the Home was co-educational.

There were also some older girls of about fourteen or fifteen who had been sent to the Bedford Home to learn domestic science and child care; they would later be put into the service of the wealthy. One of these was instructed by the matron to take care of me, which entailed kitting me out with a school uniform (such as it was) – a pair of shorts, a blue turtle-neck jersey and an ill-fitting jacket. The maid also took me to the dormitory where I would sleep. Life in the Homes had begun.

It is virtually impossible for me to record the events of the following five years or so in strict chronological order, for there are many things that I remember vividly but do not recall when exactly they happened. There are also many things that I only dimly recollect which I am unable to date precisely. I am in any event going to have my work cut out to be accurate and truthful about how I was treated, my own behaviour, and the results of it all on my life since. I will however endeavour to keep the sequence of events in reasonable continuity.

The Superintendent was a dour Scots lady with iron-grey hair brushed severely back from her forehead and tied in a bun at the nape of her neck. Her name was Miss Duke. She owned a vicious Pekinese dog which she wore around her shoulders like a mink stole. When any of the children attempted to stroke it, it snapped and snarled frantically. In those days Barnardo's autocratic policy was to bring up their children as God-fearing, hard-working, thoroughly conforming members of society. To this end the atmosphere in all of the Homes that I was in was austere, discipline was harsh – to misbehave invariably resulted in a whipping or at best some arduous task such as scrubbing floors or peeling potatoes. The institutions were run more along the lines of remand homes, borstals and prisons than cosy homes for children where love, affection and understanding were the watchwords (the image now vigorously promoted). The headmistresses were addressed as Madam and the headmasters as the Governor. I was not called by my Christian name from the time I was admitted to the Homes until the day I was discharged.

One would have thought that as the Bedford Home was specifically for 'backward' children there would have been a resident psychologist on the staff. But there was not. The method (the most apt word I can think of) for reforming educationally subnormal and emotionally disturbed children was to treat them harshly in the manner of early lunatic asylums, where insane people were tortured and beaten into submission. I am not saying that we were maltreated in the same sense, but in essence the attitude was the same. Discipline was harshly administered, rules were made not to be broken, and God had to be prayed to daily for forgiveness even if one had been good! I was well aware that the Bedford Home was for 'backward' children and in protest I would on occasions run around the lawn outside Miss Duke's window – backwards. This infuriated her greatly and she regularly applied the back of her hair-brush to my bare bottom. This was not a punishment for running backwards; the reason given was that I was out of bounds. But I did not care, indeed the worse I was treated the more I rebelled – and yet nowhere in my record does it state that I was a rebel, only that I behaved badly, and was slow at my studies, etc. Actually I do not entirely blame the administration of my day for the miserable time that I spent in the Homes, for it is self-evident that I was a pretty hopeless case long before I arrived in them. It is a shame that they did not notice this for themselves – or if they did, why did they not make some allowances for my behaviour?

Each day there were classes at which I was laboriously taught the three Rs. The alphabet I learned parrot-fashion, chanting it over and over again in my high-pitched soprano voice: 'A B C D E F G (change of key) H I J K L M N O P (repeat last five letters) L M N O P – Q – (change of key) R S T U – V – W – X – Y – Z!!' 'Once more, children,' the mistress would say, as she conducted us with a pencil as baton. I was slow to learn my three Rs, and indeed did not think that I would ever be able to master any of them – nor have I completely. It really is quite astonishing to me that when eventually I found something that I could do, it turned out to be writing. For certainly it was educationally the one thing that I was least equipped to do. How very unexpected life can be at times.

I was however good at visual things, such as art, and had in those days a great liking and aptitude for English History. There was nothing I liked better than to sit back and listen to the teacher reading grisly tales of bloody murder in the Tower of London and of corruption in high places. I could without the slightest difficulty reel off the names of all the Kings and Queens of England, also the clergy, statesmen, soldiers and sailors after only a glance at their pictures in the history books: 'Henry VIII. Captain Cook. Thomas à Becket. Bonny Prince Charlie. The Venerable Bede. The Iron Duke. Robert the Bruce. King Arthur. Oliver Cromwell. . . .' It was a game I loved to play. In this at least I was the same as any normal child, after every history lesson I would get some of the other children to enact with me the story that we had just been reading. Getting pea-sticks from the kitchen garden to use as rapiers and lumps of wood as broad-swords, the battles of Hastings and Agincourt were fought regularly in the playground after lessons. Now and then someone would get a poke in the eye with a sharp stick or a rap over the knuckles with a lump of wood, their screams of pain adding authenticity to the Wars of the Roses.

Many of the children in the Home were so mentally retarded that they spoke incoherently. It was impossible to understand one word that they uttered; others rescued by Barnardo's from conditions of appalling neglect and cruelty were stunted in their growth, there were also those who were wild and sullen, violent and unbalanced; I came into this last category. I rejected everything that they tried to do for me, I was lethargic and thoroughly anti-social, the latter being a trait that has remained with me unto this very day.

I also had quite a lot of trouble over not eating the food, which was wholesome but execrable. The day I dreaded most was Thursdays, for that was the day that we had tripe for lunch. I have since learned to consider this dish as at best an acquired taste but in those days I thought it absolutely revolting, indeed the very sight of it made me retch. There was a rule that whatever you did not eat at one meal was put before you again at the next. The guilty child was also made to stand in the cold stone passage outside the superintendent's office, holding the uneaten meal in his hand until the next mealtime. He would then be made to take his plate into the dining-room and sit with it in front of him whilst the other children ate something delicious, like bread and jam or fish cakes. I spent every Thursday afternoon standing in the passage, holding my uneaten dish of congealed tripe in my hand – but was never cured of my revulsion for it. There was one little boy who could not eat the porridge that we were given for breakfast every morning and as far as I can remember he spent his entire life standing in the passage. I was once so hungry that I stalked into the kitchen and stole a handful of raisins. Unfortunately the cook appeared and caught me red-handed as I forced them into my mouth. She immediately reported me to Miss Duke. As a punishment for my heinous crime, I was brought before the assembled school at evening prayers and was forced to drink salt water until I vomited.

One Summer's day in 1938 I fell in love with a pretty little girl with mischievous dancing black eyes; her name was Irene and she was a couple of years older than me. Our love affair began simply enough. One morning I chased her with a piece of wriggling bacon rind clasped between my forefinger and thumb – she, thinking it was a worm, ran for her life, screeching at the top of her voice. Eventually I caught her and shoved the bacon rind down the back of her neck – from that moment on we were lovers. To prove her love for me, she presented me with a string of coloured beads a day or two later which she had threaded herself. She insisted that I should wear them at all times, even at the risk of being called a sissy by the rest of the boys, which I wasn't, for I had already made something of a reputation for myself as a worthy adversary in a punch-up. (Though I was not yet the best fighter in the Home I had eliminated a few up-and-coming contenders, but a boy named Ian remained the champion; it was not until he left the Home several years later that I stepped into his shoes.)

Irene and I were sublimely happy together, she ten years old and me eight. She took care of me as though we were brother and sister. Each afternoon after classes we sat on the lawn wearing sun hats, making daisy chains. We also played a game called mothers and fathers. She, pretending that I had come home tired and hungry after a hard day's work, would serve me a make-believe tea of pretend sandwiches made of dock leaves and grass and would pour pretend tea into pretend cups adding invisible milk and sugar. Our world of make-believe was a real Elysium until one day I trod on a rusty nail which pierced the instep of my left foot. I had to be carted off to the sickbay, where I was immunized against typhoid and tetanus. I also had to stay in bed for several days, unable to walk. When after a week or so I was permitted to leave the sickbay, the impudent minx had taken up with another boy – such are the fickle ways of some women. We remained just good friends but were no longer lovers.

My anguish was, however, short-lived, for within a few days I had fallen for another girl named Hilda May who was dark and gipsy-like. With her life was mysterious. Instead of making daisy chains and taking make-believe tea on the lawn, we skulked together in the hollow of a dead oak-tree trunk, near the stagnant pond at the bottom of the meadow at the back of the kitchen garden. We collected frog-spawn and tadpoles in jamjars, minutely studied spiders' webs glistening like pearl necklaces in the morning dew. In the field there grazed a retired old cart-horse, whom we rode bareback at full speed, his mane lashing our faces as he whinnied joyfully and tossed his head in the wind. Our most gruesome sport was to catch tiny blue-winged butterflies, whose life cycle took only one day. They were born in the morning, made love in the afternoon, laid their eggs in the evening and died at nightfall. How often I have wished that the human life cycle was as brief and beautiful. The luckless ones that we caught were cut off in the prime of life, for we fed them to the swallows that wheeled overhead ever watchful for a tasty morsel. They would swoop and snatch the fluttering insects from our extended fingertips, then dart away until they became mere specks in the hazy blue sky.

Empire Day was the best and most exciting day of the year, planes from Cardington aerodrome just up the road did hair-raising stunts above our head – looping the loop in formations of six, rolling and dipping. Some daredevil pilots flew so low we ducked our heads, fearing that if we did not we would be scalped.

A fête was held on the front lawn and the games mistress organized a pageant. The boys and girls, dressed up in knitted chain mail, cardboard armour and period dresses, walked in procession around the rose-beds bearing the standard of St George, and singing: 'And did those feet in ancient time, walk upon England's mountains green. And was the Holy Lamb of God . . . etc.' at the tops of their voices, much to the delight of the visitors from the outside world, who came to give the occasion their support, spiritually and financially; they bought for a few shillings baskets we had woven in the handi-work class, jam the girls had made in the kitchen from fruit grown in the garden. There were penny rides and a slip mat that I once slid down without a mat for a dare, putting myself in the sickbay once more with my bottom full of splinters. Discipline on this day was entirely relaxed, we were permitted to do just about anything we liked; the places normally out of bounds became in bounds and the children ran riot from over-excitement, I not the least among them. But Hilda May did not like to see me make an exhibition of myself during the festivities and would summon me back to our hollow in the dead tree at the bottom of the paddock, where she would indoctrinate me with misanthropy till tea-time. But the Empire Day celebrations were always a great success and the visitors left in the early evening with their consciences salved by the knowledge that they had contributed to the survival of us poor little mites without families of our own. The trouble with these occasional breaks in our institutional routine was that it was hard to readjust oneself back to it the following morning: it would perhaps have been better not to have given us a taste of freedom at all.

There not being a chapel at the Home, we would on Sunday mornings attend the morning service at the local church, the name of which escapes me. I hated to go to church, not that I minded the service particularly. It was having to parade along the streets in a crocodile procession to and from the church that embarrassed me, for the other pedestrians always stood aside for us as we ambled by, gawping at us and whispering to one another in sympathetic tones: 'Poor little perisshers, don't they look sad?' or 'They come from the loony Home up the road. . . .' It was so arranged that we always got to the church and were seated in our pews before the arrival of the civilian congregation. I never did find out why exactly this had to be, but expect it was for no other reason than to prevent us from causing a disturbance. But to a tormented soul like mine, any treatment meted out to me that for no apparent reason differs in a single iota from that meted out to anyone else takes on the most sinister connotations in my mind. We sang hymns like mad: 'We plough the fields and scatter the good seed on the land . . .' or 'Fight the Good fight with all thy might . . .' During the long tedious sermon there was always much fidgeting, whispering and passing of notes written on the fly-leaves torn from copies of *Hymns Ancient and Modern* or the Psalms – a hair-brush offence for any vandal unfortunate enough to get caught at it. In the afternoon we went to Sunday school where we sang: 'Jesus wants me for a sunbeam,' and we were read religious allegories with stings in their tails. Though these parables were meant to be of an uplifting nature they invariably managed to put the fear of Christ into me, for without exception they were about hellfire and damnation for non-believers. To end our day of piety we would, before tea, make a pilgrimage to some local religious shrine, such as John Bunyan's place of imprisonment which was at a village near by.

One of the Bible stories that took my fancy was that of David and Goliath, and as with my fantasies about historical heroes I once got some of the boys together to act it out. The biggest boy played Goliath and the littlest played David, armed only with a dish-cloth (as a sling) and a pocketful of stones. The scene was set, the armies divided on either side of the lawn. Goliath taunted David and a good deal of convincing jeering went on on both sides. Then suddenly David placed a smooth round pebble into a corner of the dishcloth and whirled it around his head, then let fly. The stone whistled through the air miles off target, over Goliath's head and crashed through the stained-glass window depicting Jesus and several apostles. For a brief moment there was absolute silence as we stood gawping up at the gaping hole, then as though a starting-gun had been fired we ran for our lives. As we filed in for tea Miss Duke stood solemnly by the dining-room door scrutinizing every child's face as they passed by, searching for any trace of guilt. But there was such a surfeit of it that she was none the wiser when the last child had passed her by. One of the rules of the Home was that no one was permitted to sit down at the table until all the children were assembled at their places and grace had been said. The advantages of this were twofold: it meant that we would all finish our meal at more or less the same time, and it was also a good opportunity to give the assembly a lecture if they had one coming.

'Before anyone gets any tea I want the child who broke the stained-glass window to own up,' began Miss Duke, or words to that effect.

No one moved.

'I don't mind if we stand here all day,' a favourite expression of hers. 'There will be no tea until the culprit steps forward.'

Still no one moved.

Irritated by the reluctance of the guilty boy to step forward and take his punishment, Miss Duke launched into a long discourse about the violation of sacred images, in which she likened the broken light in the stained-glass window to a bad seed in a pomegranate: 'If there is one bad seed in a pomegranate it will rot the whole fruit.' So it was with the window, one broken light ruined the whole thing. For some reason that remains a complete mystery to me this peculiar simile moved the boy responsible for the damage to step forward and admit his guilt. Whereupon he was dragged off to receive his punishment and we were allowed to sit down to tea.

Christmas was always nice, we made paper chains with which we decorated the dormitories, which incidentally had such names as 'Jolly Good Company' and 'Peekaboos'. I was in the latter, a sissy name that I have not been able to live down even to this day, emotionally. We sang carols lustily: 'Come all ye faithful, have another plate full. . . .' A special effort was made in the cooking of the food and there was no standing in the passage for not eating your Christmas pudding. There were also presents (donated by charitable organizations) that were dished out by the local vicar dressed up in a Father-Christmas outfit; it was the only time in my life that I have seen Santa wearing a dog-collar. Again discipline was relaxed and we were allowed to play where we liked. The older girls, who were training to go into service, were permitted to dress themselves up in fashionable clothes and put on make-up, a very racy thing to do in those days. One young girl of about fifteen wearing bright scarlet lipstick thickly caked on her mouth once chased me into a corner and holding a sprig of mistletoe over my head, kissed me hard on the lips. I cried and squirmed in her arms begging to be let go, but she would not release me until she had completely smothered my face with the disgusting lipstick. I guess the make-up had made her feel older than her years and rather randy.

On Christmas morning after church, we were shut out of the house for an inordinately long time whilst the dining-room was prepared for the festive meal. We had snowball fights (Christmases always seemed to be white in those days) and made slides on the icy surface of the playground. The deep snow on the flower-beds outside the dining-room window came above the tops of my Wellingtons as I stood on tip-toe, my nose glued to the frosty glass, my eyes bright with excitement as I gazed at the glistening Christmas tree, the brightly coloured paper crackers set out on the tables and the candlelit crypt standing in the corner, made from an orange box and containing Jesus the Christ-child, Mary and Joseph and the three Kings bearing gifts of priceless jewels, frankincense and myrrh. All were made of Plasticine in the handiwork class and dressed in brocade robes made by the girls. What a relief it was when at last the bell rang for us to come in out of the cold and consume the Christmas fare. On ordinary days we were not permitted to speak during mealtimes (a rule strictly observed; the teachers would pace up and down the rows of tables, their ears pricked for the slightest sound other than munching). But at Christmas and the children's birthdays the rule was relaxed and the din deafening.

For many years I could not remember when my birthday was nor was I at all sure of my exact age. Oddly enough this ignorance had its advantages, for I used to celebrate my birthday whenever I felt like it, sometimes twice or even three times a year. I would simply wake up one morning and decide that today was my birthday and tell everyone to wish me many happy returns, and give me PRESENTS! Which unbelievably enough they did with what in the end amounted to monotonous regularity. By the time I had lived for eleven years I must have had something like twenty-eight birthdays. But the superindentent would only allow me one official birthday (9th June, which in fact is the actual date of my birth); however within a month or two of the party (at which we were given a cake which was cut up into pieces and had to be shared amongst all the children whether you liked them or not) I had forgotten all about it and time was ripe for another one.

I gather that in the '30s the majority of the staff in the employ of Dr Barnardo's Homes were paid only thirty pounds per annum and their keep. Whilst I am willing to agree that this meant that the vast majority of the teachers and staff had to have a sense of vocation, it was not always the case. For there were those who through lack of incentive or sheer inability did a great deal more harm than they did good. Their answer to any problem was the cane or some equal punishment; the renowned piety of the Doctor himself and his followers gave licence to the religious maniacs on the staff. Corporal punishment was sanctioned from above, even perhaps from God himself, as was mentioned to me time and again before having my backside scourged with the whip to chasten my soul in the name of divine wrath. But there was one gentle lady (whom for this I will name Miss Love) who came to the Bedford Home after I had been there a year or two. She was young, in her twenties I should think, and was incredibly beautiful; she had the sweetest, kindest face I had ever seen in my life, it was positively angelic. Her nature matched her features admirably. In the whole of my childhood in the Homes she was the only person to show me any affection or understanding. She arrived in my life on a brilliant summer's day wearing a flowered summer frock and carrying a camera. I did not at first realize that she was going to join the staff, I thought that she was just another inquisitive visitor from the outside world come to observe the antics of the infant nut cases. As with any visitor from outside the children clustered around Miss Love, their faces bright with excitement, for few of them had seen a camera before. She took one group photograph after another and told us that she would be joining the staff in a few weeks' time. I was delighted, for already I had fallen in love with her– it had been love at first sight!

Her eventual arrival was one of the high points of my life,

I had through devious channels discovered the actual date that she would be joining the staff and was waiting by the gate for her impatiently. For I wished to be the first to greet her, thereby laying first claim to her friendship. My tenacity paid dividends, for during the afternoon a car drove slowly through the gate with Miss Love sitting in the back seat. I waved frantically and she, smiling radiantly, waved back, the car drove up the gravel drive to the front door with me running alongside it (I was out of bounds but did not care). When it stopped I jerked open the door and greeted Miss Love with an elegant bow.

'Hello Miss,' I piped.

'Hello dear,' she replied, 'how nice of you to meet me.' She alighted from the car and I grabbed a small attaché case from her hand and proudly led the way into the reception hall; our relationship had begun. But what a difficult relationship it is to define exactly. I did not understand what it was that was between us then, let alone now thirty years later. Perhaps I had a mother complex about her, but certainly I never thought of her as my mother. She had an indefinable magic, a sort of aura of love and understanding; when she smiled her whole face lit up like a Christmas tree and I felt reassured and warm. Never once did I fear her, always I trusted her. Actually, though I always thought of myself as her special favourite I do not think that this was entirely true, for she treated all the children with the same tender affection; it was simply that I worked so hard at the relationship. Whenever she appeared in the playground, I would rush over to her and not leave her side until the bell had gone for classes. Ceaselessly I picked wild flowers and presented them to her, blushing profusely. And my offers of help reached noxious proportions: 'Can I clean the blackboard Miss?' 'Can I give out the exercise books Miss?' 'Can I collect the pencils Miss?' 'Shall I sweep the floor Miss?'

'Who knows where the crown jewels are kept?' Miss Love would ask.

'Me Miss,' I would blurt out, waving my hand in the air.

'Where, Norman?' she would say smiling tenderly.

'Err-um-ah Buckingham Palace,' I would reply, not having given the question the slightest thought before saying that I knew the answer. So it was with anything she asked, I was always the first to volunteer the answer, sometimes hitting on the right one more from luck than actual knowledge. And when classes were over I would always leap to my feet and charge over to the door to open it for her. Hilda May became absolutely livid, and threatened to terminate our relationship if I continued to be unfaithful to her: 'You're nothing but teacher's pet,' she said angrily. She then, as if as a punishment, gave me nits!

Nit Inspection really was one of the things that I absolutely loathed. Periodically the matron would line us up and comb our hair with a fine-toothed comb; this alone was a very painful operation for the teeth bit into the scalp and made our heads sore. But it was nothing to the ignominy of being found to be lousy. If that happened one had to suffer the indignity of having evil-smelling blue ointment rubbed into one's scalp and having to wear a towel around one's head tied up into a turban – looking for all the world like a pale-faced Sabu the Elephant Boy. I was never able to work out whether the reason for the towel was to stop the nits from jumping out onto other people or to prevent the ointment from coming off over everything. The beastly experience of having this treatment only happened to me once, but it is something that I have never forgotten, and remember always with horror. After this incident I did not have so much to do with Hilda May, not that I was no longer enamoured of her – I was – it was simply that I was petrified that she might give me nits again, or something worse. Indeed when a short time

later a wart suddenly appeared on my chin, I was absolutely
convinced that she had put a gipsy curse on me. When I had
had it for several weeks Hilda May said that if I came to the
hollow oak after school one afternoon she would exorcize the
wart and that within three days it would fall off (she did not
of course use such elevated terms). I arrived at the tree a day
or two later and glanced inside. Hilda May sat in the shadows
and looked up at me darkly, I entered and sat down beside
her on the slightly damp moss-covered ground. After in-
specting the wart she left the hollow and ran to the old horse
happily grazing near by and plucked a thread from its mane.
Returning to the tree she tied the horsehair around the base
of the wart and pulled it as tightly as she could; it was painful
but bearable. Sure enough within three days the wart fell
off. At the time I was certain that Hilda May had spirited
it away. Of course what had actually happened was that the
horsehair had cut off the blood circulation to the growth and
it had died of strangulation, at least that is what Miss Love
said when I told her about the magical happening.

I am certain that it was through the kindness of Miss
Love that I began to improve in my behaviour and school
work, also I became far less sullen. Indeed in a report to
the General Superintendent of Barnardo's Miss Duke wrote
of my progress: '*Behaviour:* Good. *Progress at School:* Fair.
*Habits:* Clean. Improving very slowly.'

One day Miss Love gave each of the children in her class
a sunflower seed and said that we were each to plant them
separately in a long row in a flower-bed in the garden. Each
child was to write his or her name on a marker and push it
into the ground next to their seed. The reason for this was
that there was to be a sunflower race, with prizes for the first
three tallest. Each morning after breakfast there was a mad
rush for the flower-bed to see if any of the seeds were giving

off shoots. For weeks nothing at all happened. Frustrated by the time that the seeds were taking to sprout, some of us dug up ours to see how they were progressing, thus stunting their growth even further. But soon the shoots began to appear, and the race was really on. Each child nurtured his own personal sunflower as though it were a human, watering it daily, and dung from the old horse in the paddock was at a premium. Having once begun to grow the plants soon gathered momentum, the ones that had been left to nature and not dug up for inspection had a head start and before long began to outstrip the others. Competition was keen and there was much excitement as the competitors measured their stems each day with a tape measure, Miss Love acting as judge and also keeping an ever-watchful eye to see that there was no foul play – such as the changing over of markers by cheats whose sunflowers were stunted. Eventually the tallest burst into flower; the rules were that when the tallest sunflower was in full bloom the race would be over. When the great day arrived Irene, from whom I had now been enstranged for several months, won first prize – a bag of sweets. I swiftly re-instated myself as her lover for the rest of the afternoon, until the bag was empty. Then I returned to Hilda May, who had no interest in such things as sweets and cultivated flowers; her passion was for wild flowers and blackberries, which were liable to give you worms or diarrhœa.

In the kitchen garden Hilda May and I collected green caterpillars and kept them in matchboxes together with a piece of cabbage leaf; our hope was that they would turn into chrysalises and then butterflies, but metamorphosis did not take place, match-boxes not being their natural habitat I suppose. Also in the garden there were two pigs living in a sty. I was absolutely terrified of them (Hilda May, needless to say, was not) and always gave the sty a wide birth whenever I was compelled to pass it. Hilda May would jeer at me and call me a coward but no taunt would induce me to go near those pigs. They lived on swill from the kitchen and absolutely anything else that was thrown into the sty, such as coal and string. Once I even saw them cannibalistically gnawing on a side of bacon that had gone bad and been thrown away.

In the summer the gardens were beautiful and fragrant, in those days the summers always seemed to be long and hot and the flowers grew in great profusion. There were hollyhocks as tall as a man, lupins, pansies, peonies, snapdragons, chrysanthemums and a multitude of others, all of them living up to their pretty tinkling names. There was one punishment that I greatly enjoyed and that was weeding the flower-beds. Whenever I was caught doing something wrong I would always say: 'I don't care what you do to me, so long as you don't make me weed the flower-beds.' I had of course taken the idea from the fables of Joel Chandler Harris about Brer Rabbit and Brer Fox: 'Whatever you do don't throw me into the briar patch,' said the Rabbit one day when he had been caught by the Fox, whereupon the Fox threw him straight into the briar patch thinking that it would be the thing most painful to the poor Rabbit, but of course it was the Rabbit's favourite place on earth – so it was with me and the flower-beds. And sure enough it worked like a charm; through various bits of bad behaviour I was made to sit among the flowers minutely observing their aesthetic beauty and now and then pulling up bits of chickweed and deadly nightshade just to show willing.

Hilda May was very greatly given to losing her temper, indeed when riled she became a raving maniac. Her temper was also extremely unpredictable, for more often than not it took only a small irritation to set her off. I well remember one occasion we had been sitting in the hollow oak smoking Old Man's Beard, white flaxen weed the real name of which escapes me, (it is however worth mentioning that it has no hallucinatory properties whatever, indeed all it does is make you cough a lot). I had several times gone to Miss Love's house in the town for tea (she, unlike the rest of the staff, did not live in), and Hilda May was very cross about this for she rightly felt that Miss Love was alienating my affections. Innocently, I made some remark about what a nice time I had had at one of Miss Love's tea parties; no sooner had I said this than I wished I had bitten my tongue off instead, for Hilda May flew into a blind rage the ferocity of which left me numb with fear. She rampaged around the inside of the hollow tree screaming at the top of her voice, not abuse, just screams. It was a very unnerving experience. Suddenly she picked up a pile of comics belonging to me and tore them to pieces, screaming all the while. I was frightened that she would be heard by a member of the staff, who would be bound to think that I had done Hilda May some terrible injury – suddenly I sprang to my feet and put my hand over her mouth in an attempt to stifle the noise. Her teeth sank into my little finger and I let out an excruciating shriek of pain, louder and even more piercing than hers were now, for she was becoming exhausted. Eventually she let go of my finger and calmed down, but forever after that I was frightened of her. Poor Hilda May, she was not just mentally deficient like the rest of us, she was entirely deranged. I tied a piece of rag around my finger, and did not go to the sickbay to have it dressed for I could not think of a plausible enough excuse to give the matron about how it had happened. Two days later my finger had swollen up to about double its normal size and was festering where the skin was broken. In the end I had to go sick; I do not remember how I explained the wound but certainly I did not tell the truth – to have done so would have meant being branded a 'tell-tale' for evermore.

When the war broke out in 1939 there was much excitement at the Home and much activity at Cardington Aerodrome just up the road. Tanks, Bren-gun-carriers and huge army lorries packed with soldiers lumbered by the gates of the Abbey, for days the convoys roared by in an endless stream, the soldiers singing 'Roll out the barrel,' 'Run rabbit, run rabbit, run, run, run,' and 'Take me back to dear old Blighty,' songs which were in those days more patriotic even than the National Anthem. Miss Duke allowed us to pick fruit for the soldiers in the orchard, for which they gave us pennies; it was just an exchange of presents for we were certainly not in business. But the money was nice to have just the same, for I cannot remember ever seeing any before the few coppers thrown to us by the Tommies. We waved wildly as they went by and wished them luck. I was convinced that the war was going on just up the road at the Aerodrome – shades of my history lessons perhaps, where opposing armies faced each other in a field and fought bravely until the weaker side was vanquished; what a romantic I was. (As a matter of fact I still feel that this would be the best way of solving the differences between one country and another. All the generals and politicians of both sides should meet on neutral ground and fight it out, without involving the populace. I doubt if that is a very original thought, but it would make a good TV spectacle.)

As the battle raged in Europe, our classes took an interesting turn. A large map of the continent was pinned to the wall of the classroom, and each day the mistress stuck little flags on it, black for the Germans and red for the Allies, to denote the progress of each. I was quite certain that the Germans would win the war, as the Axis forces conquered one European country after another. The map became a mass of black flags and hardly a red one in sight. On days that I was feeling particularly badly treated, I wished that the Germans would hurry, for I felt sure they would release me from my torment. We listened to Winston Churchill's speeches on the radio, and were told by Miss Duke that all would be well so long as he was running things. She was at least right in that.

The Blitz raged in London during 1940-41 and Barnardo's head office at Stepney suffered damage, but we never heard a sound. Our lives continued much the same, rural and peaceful. The alarming news bulletins meant nothing to me, nor did the dreadful headlines of our soldiers being killed, for I was still unable to read. Spitfires and bombers took off from Cardington Aerodrome the whole time and flew overhead, but no enemy aircraft got as far as Bedford. It not being an industrial town, I suppose the Luftwaffe saw no reason to waste any bombs on it.

It was from Cardington Aerodrome that the ill-fated airship R 101 took off for India but crashed in France; there were only six survivors. That was in the early thirties. After the tragedy airships were scrapped and Cardington Aerodrome became just about non-operational, excepting for the Empire Day air displays. But now it was having a new lease of life and was a hive of activity. There was much coming and going of impressive-looking staff cars carrying high officials, battalions of troops were on the move marching three abreast, grim-faced with rifles on their shoulders, dispatch riders roared by on motorcycles to and fro. We had fire drill two or three times a week: to me this could not have been more terrifying had it been the real thing, for I suffer from vertigo. The fire drills consisted of being lowered from the topmost window of the building in a sort of harness arrangement. We were made to line up and each child was lowered to the ground one after the other; without fail I was always the last to go, and indeed would try to avoid the ordeal if I possibly could. But I was by this time the toughest and most senior boy in the Home so I had therefore to put a brave face on it.

With the advent of food rationing the margarine on our bread was spread even more thinly than usual, but apart from that we were virtually unaffected by it, for we had few luxuries at the best of times. Never were we given more food than was needed to keep us fit and well, so now that the whole country were being asked to tighten their belts, we were in good condition for the deprivation without having to make the patriotic effort.

Some of the children from Barnardo's were sent to America and Australia for safety's sake, several went from the Bedford Home but I was not among them. I desperately wanted to go for anything, I felt, would be better than my present circumstances. Whilst the selection board at head office were deliberating on who should go, I suddenly became astonishingly adept at geography. I studied the school atlas for hours together and memorized most of the capitals of the world. I also told Miss Love on alternate days that I wanted either to be a sheep-farmer or a cowboy, but my efforts were to no avail, for when the names were called one morning at breakfast mine was not among them. And in the weeks that followed my interest in geography went into a steep decline.

About this time everyone seemed certain that a German invasion was imminent and we were warned that there were liable to be a lot of German spies about, we were also instructed never to speak to strangers. The government slogan was: 'CARELESS TALK COSTS LIVES.' But there wasn't really anyone to whom we could carelessly talk, except each other. It was all very exciting, everyone I saw that I did not know became a potential spy and so did many of the people that I did know, in particular the gardener, who had been an enemy of mine since long before war had been declared. He once reported me for standing up on the seat of the swing in the playground, a grave offence, I remember. His every move became suspicious to me. When he went into the

Goldings

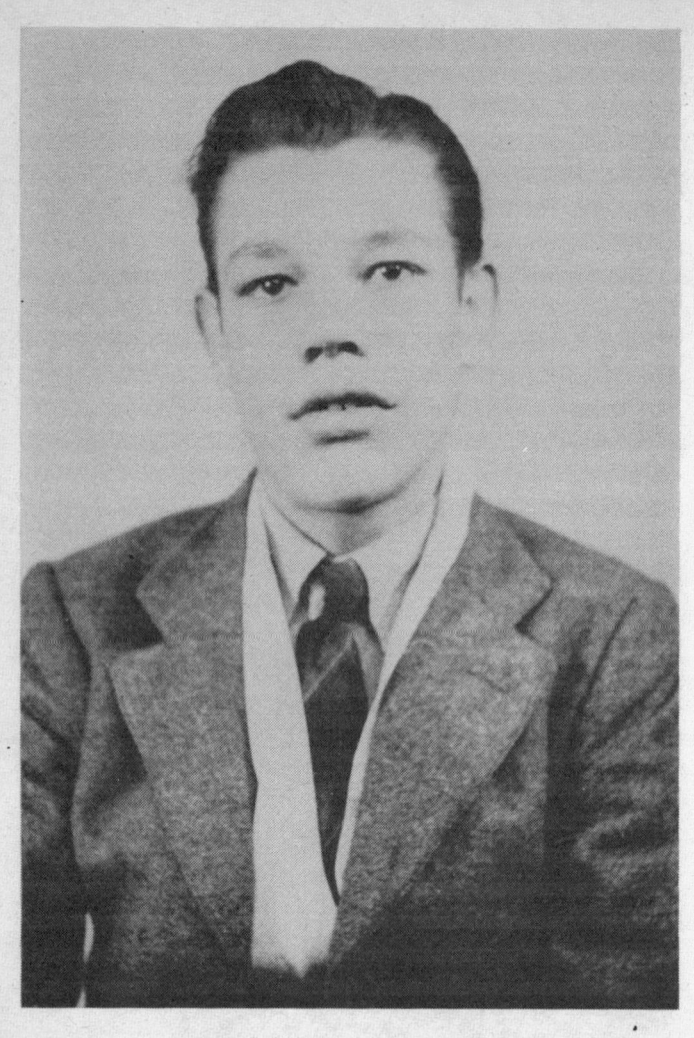

The 'Situation Photograph'. The last day, aged sixteen

garden shed for his tea and sandwiches I would stalk through the giant cabbages with the stealth of an Indian scout, and upon reaching the shed I would peer darkly at him through the tiny window at the back. His every move took on sinister connotations – his newspaper became secret plans, his tea-pot a booby trap, his tool-chest a two-way receiver. One day I conveyed my suspicions to Miss Love, who to my great disappointment only smiled and told me not to be so silly, whereupon I became very irritable and insistent. Miss Love soothed me with kind words and in the end agreed to report the matter to the head of Counter-Espionage. But to my intense dissatisfaction nothing whatever happened and Von Schicklgruber (my name for him) continued as the gardener for the duration, undetected except by me, and is there yet as far as I know. But I expect he has gone over to the Communists by now.

One day an old boy from the Home now in his teens paid us a visit wearing an army uniform; he was on embarkation leave and would be off to the front shortly. Miss Duke introduced him to us at morning assembly and spoke of him in glowing terms, we in our turn gawped at him admiringly. 'He is a hero of the British Empire,' she said, her tone deathly earnest, at which the young man became bashful and shuffled his feet – what an ordeal it must have been for him especially as he may only have been just another reluctantly conscripted soldier. When Miss Duke had finished her highly complimentary sermon, we all bowed our heads and said a prayer for him. I wonder how he fared in the battles. I truly hope that he came through it all unscathed, for his extreme youth and innocent expression made a profound impression on me at the time, despite the fact that he was quite a few years older than me. He fired in me a hitherto lacking sense of national pride. I became loyal to the cause of freedom and began to salute the officers in command of the troops that passed the gate. I was bitterly disappointed that I was not old enough to go to war myself. (In later life when I was old enough to fight for my country in Malaya, Korea and other points East I had not the slightest inclination to do so, nor did I.)

The winter of 1940 was particularly severe, it snowed heavily and was bitterly cold, the conditions were such that they greatly hampered the war effort, the convoys got snowed under and things at Cardington Aerodrome came to a virtual standstill. After several weeks there came the thaw and the river Ouse which flows through Bedfordshire burst its banks. Houses were flooded and the water was deep enough in the streets to float rowing boats – indeed for a time this was the only means of transport. The Home was completely cut off by flood; we were however luckier than many for the water only surrounded the building like a moat but did not come inside. We all loved every minute of the siege and paddled about in the water like ducks despite repeated orders not to, but our disobedience went unpunished because the staff had their work cut out keeping the place afloat, let alone anything else.

The fire brigade tried desperately to pump the water away, with little success, for the more they pumped the higher the water seemed to rise. A favourite pastime during the great flood was walking tightrope along the boundary wall at the front of the Abbey; it was quite a precarious feat and not entirely devoid of danger for the mud and slime from the recent weather had made the surface extremely slippery. Though the wall was not very high, it was certainly high enough for a small child to break a limb if he fell off. 'Betcha I can do it quicker than you!' one boy would shout. 'Betcha can't,' another would reply. And the race was on to see who could cover the distance from end to end the soonest, a distance of some fifty yards though it may have been shorter, for things look twice their actual size to children. One boy after another mounted the wall, some treading gingerly for fear that they might fall, others charging at top speed, throwing caution to the winds.

'Let me have a go,' piped a little girl's voice.

'This ain't a game for girls,' shouted one of the boys.

'I bet I could do it faster than any of you,' she insisted.

'Betcha, can't!'

I looked to see who the girl was and was not entirely surprised to see Hilda May mounting the wall at the far end.

'You'll fall,' shouted someone.

'Of course I won't,' laughed Hilda May and began to skip along the top of the wall like a fairy; somewhere near the middle she wobbled slightly but did not lose her balance, we all let out a gasp. Without the slightest fear or hesitation she covered the rest of the distance like a circus performer and climbed down at the other end amid thunderous applause and deafening cheers. Though none of us had a watch (or were able to read the time if we had) it was unanimously agreed that she had made the fastest time and was the outright winner of the competition. Hilda May ignored the congratulations and walked away triumphantly with her tiny snub nose in the air.

As I have intimated earlier, our lives were affected by the war hardly at all, certainly in no serious way. We were asked not to waste or throw anything away, such as silver paper, comics, food and even bottles, for all these things, we were told, were of immense importance to the war effort. Though I must own that I was amazed that things like the *Dandy*, *Beano* and *Film Fun* were of any use to the war effort, later I found out that waste paper was made into pulp and then into paper again, which explained matters considerably. Now and then the ARP paid us a visit to see that the fire extinguishers were in good order and that the black-out curtains showed no chinks of light. There also seemed now to be far less activity at the aerodrome and not nearly so many lorries filled with troops passed the gate. So quite naturally I took it for granted that the war was now over, though I had not the slightest idea who had won it, and cannot honestly say that I gave the matter very much thought, or in fact any thought at all.

Our schooling continued uninterrupted by the global holocaust, and during our free time we still idled away the hours playing fivestones, hop-scotch, conkers and war games. Where once our battles had been historic, now there was much yelling of 'Heil Hitler!' and little boys roared around the playground, their arms outstretched like wings and going: 'Aaaaaaaaaahhrrrrr – Ppppuuughchchch!!!' as they impersonated dive bombers. There was also a good deal of hiding behind trees, walls and: 'Bang bang! You're dead.'

'I am not.'

'Yes you are.'

'No I'm not!'

'Yes you are, if you don't fall down I'm not playing with you any more.' Followed by tears perhaps and shouts of:

'Cowardy, cowardy custard!'

'No I'm not, you're dead anyway.'

'You're M.D.'

'If I am you are.'

'I'm going to tell on you.'

'Tell tale tit your tongue will split.'

'No it won't, you're dead.'

'So are you, bang bang!'

'That's not fair, I wasn't expecting it.'

'Don't care if you weren't. Bang bang! You really are dead now.'

'It's not fair.'

''Course it is.'

'No it isn't. I'm not playing with you any more ever.'
'Don't care.'
'Yes you do.'
'No I don't.'
'Don't care was made to care.'
The general would stride over and intervene:
'What's up with you two?' he would demand to know.
'He's dead but he won't lie down. . . .'
'I'm not I got you first.'
'Oooo you are a fibber.'
'No I'm not.'
'I'm never going to speak to you again.'
'Don't care if you don't.'
'Yes you do.'
'If I say I don't I don't, *see*!'

With luck the bell would then ring, summoning us to tea and ending the potentially ugly scene.

I had now been at the Bedford Home for about four years and was the senior boy at the school. This did not entail many privileges but there were a few. I was sometimes allowed to go to the shops with Miss Love to buy sweets for the other children; for a farthing you could buy a Black Jack which was a square of black toffee about an inch across that had the appearance and consistency of a tart and was about as appetizing – but it was in those days my favourite sweet, though I was also rather partial to sherbert. Gobstoppers were two for a farthing and lasted for ages so long as you didn't suck them too hard. There were also triangular fruit-flavoured ices a penny each, chemically flavoured blackcurrant juice a halfpenny a bottle, to be drunk on the premises because of the bottle shortage – the sweetshop man trusted no one. There were sticky lollipops that I liked and liquorice sticks that I hated and still do. Broken biscuits could sometimes be got from the grocer – a penny for a huge bagful.

'Have you got any broken biscuits today?' I would ask the man behind the counter.

'Sorry sonny not today,' he would sometimes say.

'Well, why don't you break some then!' I would retort.

In spite of Miss Love's good influence, I remained a difficult child. The slightest thing would set me back considerably and I would become withdrawn and sullen. I needed desperately to be loved and wanted and yet I did every mortal thing to prevent anyone from doing so. I demanded that the people who liked me should dance attendance on me morning, noon and night. When I did not get my own way I would throw a tantrum the vehemence of which would have blackened the heart of an angel against me. But Miss Love was always kind and sympathetic no matter how badly I behaved. Often I would try her patience to the limit through sheer cussedness, but I think she saw through my little game and completely ignored me, which needless to say only served to infuriate me the more.

Miss Love started a tambourine band and though I had no ear for music I demanded that I should be in it. The children would sing whilst the tambourine players beat a tinkling rhythm – there were no other instruments in the band. Perhaps somewhat reluctantly, Miss Love agreed that I should be in the band, but my sense of timing and rhythm was so bad that I volunteered to give it up through sheer embarrassment. As I walked away thoroughly dejected Miss Love called me back, and handing me her baton invited me to have a go at conducting the other children. I stood on a wooden box, wild with excitement, and began to wave the stick about with the zest of a young Stravinsky. To my utter astonishment my performance was a great success, the more wildly I waved my arms about the louder the children sang and banged their tambourines. I had got the job as school conductor! Sometimes when the choir became hoarse, Miss Love would put a record on the battered old wind-up gramophone standing in the corner and to the accompaniment of the tambourine band I would wildly conduct *Tiger Rag* or *Alexander's Rag-Time Band*. I was really in my element and leapt and shouted for joy as I waved my arms about in a frenzy – spurring the tambourine-bashers on to greater and even greater effort. Actually, though I was greatly exhilarated by the jazz numbers, my favourite song in those days was *Where'er you Walk*. What my performance on the dais lacked in expertise it made up for in exuberance. Indeed one afternoon Miss Love invited the Superintendent and various other members of the staff to one of our recitals. Proudly I mounted my soap-box and began to throw myself about in such a lunatic fashion that I am certain some members of the audience must have thought that at any moment I would have apoplexy. But I gesticulated my way through half a dozen numbers with titles like *Lovely Canada, Rule Britannia,* and *The Quartermaster's Stores* (an Army song that we had picked up from the soldiers as they marched past the gate). There were some rather risqué alternatives to some of the verses but for this recital we stuck to the clean ones; to finish off with we sang two rousing choruses of the National Anthem. The audience applauded enthusiastically and Miss Duke complimented me on my performance and said that the whole thing had been most entertaining. I was filled with transcendent pride and bowed low in humble fashion several times from the waist. My popularity as a conductor led me to believe that I really knew something about music – a boy wonder in fact: this of course was totally untrue, my success stemmed only from the fact that I was prepared to make a spectacle of myself in public. Nevertheless the general appreciation of my self-expression gave me confidence in other directions and my behaviour and school work began to improve slightly. The encouragement of members of the staff, Miss Love in particular, was a tonic to my addled brain.

The most frowned-upon crime at the Bedford Home was bed-wetting; it was also the most prolifically committed. Great moral judgments were showered upon offenders, and the dreadful punishment inflicted by the matron when she came around on early-morning inspection was rubbing the children's noses in their urine-soaked sheets, as though they were animals. The same punishment was meted out to both girls and boys. None of them could help it, but all were treated as though they did it on purpose. There was one little girl who wet the bed almost every night in spite of the fact that she was woken up and taken to the lavatory twice and sometimes three times. Each morning the matron would enter the dormitory where she slept and tear the sheets from her bed. The little girl would scream in terror and plead for mercy, but it availed her nothing, the matron would grab hold of her, pinioning her arms and up-ending her face-first into the sopping sheet. Though this unceremonious treatment cured no one it was never abolished. Though it was rarer, one or two of the children were occasionally given to 'messing' the bed as well as wetting it, the punishment for this was the same accompanied by a thrashing and a dose of senna pods. It was said that if you touched a dandelion it would make you wet the bed, I was always too frightened to find out if there was any truth in it.

As a rule the girls and boys slept in separate dormitories but sometimes through overcrowding, or when one of the dormitories was being redecorated, we had to co-habit the same rooms. None of us had reached the age of puberty so there were no worries on that score, that is to say no worries as far as the staff were concerned. On one such occasion I slept in a bed next to a girl whose name I have completely forgotten. It was a summer evening and still light outside, the birds sang in the trees and a heady perfume drifted through the window from the azalea bushes in the garden. We whispered secret thoughts and stifled our giggles in our pillows and then suddenly she brazenly said: 'If you show me yours I'll show you mine' – her exact words. I knew very well what she meant from our previous conversation; simultaneously we threw back our bed covers and I untied my pyjama cord whilst she lifted her nightie. There we lay both entirely exposed, she observing my tiny cock and I her hairless little mound. It was not a pornographic act, but merely childish curiosity; perhaps it was latently sexual but if so we were entirely unaware of it. If was the first flower of virginity that I ever saw (though I cannot say that I knew what I was looking at, or what it was for) and I have not seen a prettier one since. For the next few days I suffered great guilt over the incident and avoided the girl as though she had the plague. She too, I think, suffered a little of the same, for on the odd occasions that we could not shun each other, such as meal-times and during classes, she would lower her eyes and blush.

I did not mention our guilty secret to a soul, certainly not to Hilda May whose maidenhood I had never seen, for fear that she would become jealous and throw one of her tantrums. Or worse she might have demanded that I inspect hers as well, thus making me into a sex maniac before my time.

There was a boy at the Home named Fat Pat who, though he was only ten or eleven, weighed almost as much as a grown man, nine stone perhaps. He was very stupid and had a harelip which enhanced his repulsive appearance greatly. I was always thoroughly rotten to him for no reason whatever and as a result he stayed out of my way as much as possible. One day I made some beastly and totally unfair remark to him: to my utter astonishment, he did not run away near to tears as was usual but stood his ground and defiantly insulted me back. Incensed by this unprecedented turn of events I flew at him, fists clenched, and began to pummel his fat body. He fell to the ground and rolled himself into a ball, his head between his knees and his hands over his ears for added protection. I ferociously followed up my initial advantage by leaping on top of him and continuing the onslaught, but my rain of tiny blows was almost totally ineffectual, for Pat's fat acted as a protective armour, the harder I punched the less damage I seemed to do. It was like punching a great rubber mattress, for my fists bounced off him like tennis balls off a wall. After several minutes I got out of breath and completely exhausted. He must have sensed that I was tiring for suddenly he reared up like an enraged elephant and sent me sprawling on the ground several feet away. Seizing this heaven-sent opportunity for revenge he landed on top of me like a ton of bricks, knocking the last breath of wind from my lungs. And as I lay there gasping he clouted my face with his podgy fists until my nose bled and my eyes were blackened. At last he stopped, got off me and ran away, leaving me where I lay, a sorry sight. The other children clustered around and looked down at my huddled frame in astonished silence; the champion had been defeated. Fat Pat was now the governor of the Home. Well, not quite, for when I had recovered from my salutory lesson, I without the slightest hesitation demanded a return bout, which rotund Pat adamantly refused to oblige me with. However, I was extremely wary of him forever after that and no longer insulted him. Not I think from fear as much as now having a sneaking regard for him, but it would have been more than my slightly tarnished reputation was worth to mention that to a soul, so I didn't.

Month followed month and year followed year uneventfully, just the same old institutional routine, day in day out. Get up, wash, make your bed, sweep the floor, breakfast, PT, morning prayers, classes, lunch, play, classes, play, tea, mow the lawn, play, evening prayers (God bless all except the wall) bed, sleep. Except for Sundays the only way to tell which day of the week it was was by what we were getting for lunch. Monday: Mince. Tuesday: Toad in the Hole. Wednesday: Bacon. Thursday: Tripe (ugh!). Friday: Fish. Saturday: Shepherd's pie. Sunday: Roast meat. The menu never changed from one year's end to the next, but we seemed to thrive on it, though perhaps it would be better to say we survived on it. When I was eleven a decision had to be made on my progress at the Abbey. If satisfactory I would be sent to a Boy's Home, if not, to a Senior School for Educationally Subnormal Boys. On 21st August 1941 I was sent to Barnardo's Home at Kingston-upon-Thames which would indicate that I was no longer thought to be mentally backward, though a note states: 'Educationally still some way to go.'

When I first heard that I was 'Going away' I became very excited, but was not as delighted as might be supposed. I hated the idea of being parted from Miss Love and though there were many things that I did not like about the place, I had long become accustomed to them. It was like being uprooted all over again. At Kingston I was a 'new boy' again; where at Bedford I had been the oldest I was now to be the youngest and weakest.

On the day before I left Miss Love took me out to a bumper feast at a tea-house in the town. We were both sad and taciturn as we sat facing each other across the heavily laden table. I think we both knew that we were unlikely ever to see or hear from one another again. But we did not cry, indeed we tried desperately to stay cheerful and I munched my way through as many cucumber sandwiches and cream cakes as I could. On the morning of my departure Miss Love hugged and kissed me tenderly and instructed me to be a good boy and do what I was told. The bravely held back tears then poured out in a torrent. Miss Love comforted me and bribed me with a piece of silver to be spent on the journey, whereupon I bucked up and set off amid a flurry of handkerchief-waving and shouts of 'Good-bye, and I'll come and see you when I grow up.' I heard that Miss Love took over as Superintendent some years later upon the death of Miss Duke, so perhaps the next generation of little people had a better time of it than I did.

For the life of me I cannot remember how I was transported from Bedford to Kingston, which is very much a cross-country journey. By rail I would have had to come to London, change stations and catch another train to Kingston. I remember none of that, so it seems more likely that I went by road. In any event coming to London in those days was an extremely hazardous business, for one stood an excellent chance of being caught in an air-raid and blown to bits by a German bomb. So it seems doubly likely that I made the trip across country by road, for safety's sake.

# *Kingston*

THERE WERE A GOOD MANY DIFFERENCES between the two Homes. Kingston was far less rural, there were only boys there, the staff were almost entirely male though there was one house matron who took care of the clothes and the younger boys. There was also a nursing sister who took care of our ailments. The Superintendent, known officially as the Governor, was named Mr Gardener. Of all the people I met in the Homes, he remains the most difficult to fathom. He smoked voraciously, and seemed only interested in the band and Brentford football team (it was advisable to give him a wide berth when the team had lost a match of a Saturday afternoon). He left the running of the place to the rest of the staff and I saw him rarely.

But the greatest difference between the Bedford and Kingston Homes was that at the latter we went to an outside school. It was at this school that the real stigma of being brought up in an orphanage was made clear to me. There were many fights with the 'outside' boys, who also went to the school, particularly when they referred to us as 'Dr Banana Boys!' We were also rather looked down on by the teachers and parents. If there was ever any trouble (which there almost always was) we invariably got the blame for it. I think this was mainly because we were usually responsible for it.

The war was now at a critical stage: the sirens wailed almost every day, warning us of enemy aircraft overhead. To be caught without your gas mask was a punishable offence, and fire drill was as regular as going to church on Sundays. We learned how to use a stirrup-pump and spent a good deal of our time in air-raid shelters. Any progress that I might have made at Bedford was soon lost; I came bottom of the class in just about every subject in the curriculum. Instead of being mentally retarded I now became a nasty little boy, always in trouble and hating everyone I came into contact with, both boys and staff. I was savagely beaten times without number, the punishment which at Bedford had always been administered to my backside now moved to my hands. During my three years there I was caned so often my arithmetic was never good enough to keep count. On one occasion I was given a stinging stroke of the cane on each hand for being a couple of minutes late for school, actually it was almost a daily ritual for I was late at least four out of five days in a week. But this particular morning it was bitterly cold, which made the pain doubly hard to bear, for my fingers were already numb from the icy wind. In pique I suddenly turned on the master and snarled: 'When I grow up I'm going to come back here and kill you!' But I never did and I expect he is dead anyway by now, for he was quite an old man then (all the young teachers had gone off to the war). Of course my remark was reported to the governor of the Home, who gave me another thrashing that evening.

There were about two hundred boys at the Home (maybe a few less) their ages ranging between eleven and fourteen, which in those days was school-leaving age. At fourteen many were found situations and let out into the world to fend for themselves, while others were sent to technical college to learn a trade. The Home could therefore be looked upon as a place between junior school and grammar-school, but in fact all it was was a house full of boys being kept as safely as possible from the dangers of war. This of course was no fault of Barnardo's, but us kids who were later to be known as 'products of the war' suffered for it greatly. Though few bombs were actually dropped on Kingston there were many air-raid warnings and a good deal of our time was spent in air-raid shelters. Therefore we received very little schooling though we attended classes every day, for almost as soon as we were seated at our desks, the siren would go and down we would march into the bowels of the earth in orderly fashion, safe from all but a direct hit.

My greatest ambition at the Kingston Home was to join the band, and learn to play the bagpipes. I applied to the governor several times but was always turned down flat, despite the fact that I had been a dab hand with the baton in Miss Love's tambourine band a year or two before. Instead I got all the terrible jobs. I built flower-bed walls with clinkers from the furnace and was then made to whitewash them. For a time I was put to work in the lavatory: every day I washed down the urinals with foul-smelling disinfectant that was so strong that it burnt your hands. I would then scrub the floor with a yard broom. One day the cook found out that the same broom was being borrowed from the lavatory to scrub the mud from the potatoes, which were always steamed and served up in their jackets because the skins were said to be good for us. My own opinion is that they merely wished to save the trouble of peeling them. The handle of the lavatory broom was immediately painted red, in order that the same mistake would not happen again, if indeed mistake it was.

One morning I found one of the lavatory pans blocked with excrement, and full to the brim with foul water. The master in charge took one look at it and then at me: 'Come on lad!

Don't just stand there!' he bellowed. 'Get your hand down there and fish it out! It's all your own!' It was my command performance of the war.

One day six Spanish boys arrived at the Home in a coach; they were refugees from the Spanish civil war, and the British Government had asked Barnardo's if they would take them into their care. None of the boys could speak a word of English; there therefore sprang up a great communications problem between them and us. But they were a lively bunch and I greatly liked their swarthy complexions and flashing smiles. They always went around together and inadvertently broke many of the rules through not being able to understand the language, such as the rule forbidding talking at meal-times, which irritated the masters somewhat, but delighted me beyond belief.

One day I was lounging about in the gymnasium enviously watching some of the bigger boys swinging hand over hand along the steel bars that spanned the roof. I was still far too puny to attempt such feats of daring, and in any case my vertigo would not have cared for the idea overmuch.

Suddenly the Spanish boys appeared in the doorway and for a time stood watching the antics of the would-be Tarzans as they swung about. Then one of them muttered something to another and they all began to laugh. The bigger boys up on the bars, thinking that they were being ridiculed, began to shout abusive remarks at the refugees, who in reply merely laughed for they had not the slightest idea what was being said to them. Then without warning one of them who was about the same size and age as me stepped forward and, taking a firm grip on the thick rope (that was the only route to the bars), shinned up it like greased lightning and began to swing about like a monkey. His dexterity was such that he put even the best of the school athletes to shame as he swung from one bar to another with wonderful grace and precision. So flabbergasted were the other gymnasts that (not wanting to be shown up) they stopped trying to compete with him and came down to the floor where they stood gaping up at him with their mouths hanging open. After a while the Spanish boy, having made his point, slid down the rope to the floor, his face gleaming with sweat and wreathed in smiles. Then as though to add insult to injury he ran several paces, leapt off the ground and did a somersault in mid-air. He landed lightly on his feet like a panther, grinned at his astonished audience, caught my eye and winked, then proudly joined his compatriots and strutted out of the door. I resolved then and there that this was someone whose friend I was going to be. How I was going to manage it I had not the slightest idea, I just hoped that something would come up to make it happen, if not I would do something to make it happen.

During this time there was still some talk about a German invasion, though less than there had been the year before. In preparation or perhaps anticipation of this eventuality various precautionary measures were being taken. Pillboxes were being built at vantage points around the countryside and barbed wire was being put down all over the place. On every conceivable stretch of land where a troop-carrying glider might land deep trenches were dug. The boys from the Home helped the civilian population dig them. Sandbags by the thousand had to be filled, salvage had to be collected and taken to the Civil Defence depot, socks and Balaclava helmets which had been knitted by the WVS had to be packed and sent to the soldiers at the front, and German spies had still to be looked out for – in all these things we 'did our bit'.

Now and then bombers would fly over *en route* for Berlin, sometimes they were so thick in the sky that they blotted out the sun. There were too the occasional stray Messerschmitt 109s that had by some freak of circumstance taken the wrong way home; Spitfires harassed them mercilessly. Watching dogfights was a rare treat and I always ignored the matron's comments of: 'Come inside this instant, do you want to get killed?' for I knew that she would be too frightened to come and make me. One day I even saw one shot down: two Spitfires buzzed around it like hornets, there were distant bursts of machine-gun fire, so far off that they sounded no louder than cap guns. Suddenly a black plume of smoke came out of the tail of the Messerschmitt, the engine began to splutter and it went into a nose-dive (just like on the films) the pilot parachuted out and his plane crashed in a field several miles away and blew up. The pilot I suppose was captured by a farmer, and marched to the headquarters of the Home Guard at the point of a pitchfork. In those days the Home Guard trained with broomsticks, for all the rifles were needed by the soldiers at the front.

Not far away there was a prisoner-of-war camp, the prisoners being mostly if not entirely Italian. They worked on the land picking potatoes and planting cabbages. They were a friendly crowd and never caused any trouble, on the contrary they were very co-operative and were greatly trusted by their guards. On Saturday afternoons some of them were allowed out of the camp and permitted to wander around the town freely. The local girls seemed very attracted to them and there was a good deal of *rapporto sessuale* behind the bushes, till one teenage landgirl got pregnant and gave birth to a bouncing little *ragazzo*. Whereupon there was a great outcry from her parents and the prisoners' freedom was greatly curtailed.

From 1944 we really came under attack from Doodle-Bugs and V 2 rockets. One day a Doodle-Bug came 'pop-pop-popping' across the sky. Suddenly the engine stopped directly overhead. Most of the boys dived for cover, but I stood gawping up at it, mesmerized as it glided softly down towards me, narrowly missing the bell tower of the Home.

It crashed in a field less than a mile away and exploded, like a mighty thunderclap, blowing every window out of the Home and me off my feet. Later we were allowed to go and see the crater, which to me at the time seemed to be the size of a football pitch.

Due to the dangers of being in the house we slept in the air-raid shelter whether the warning had sounded or not. But the dug-out which the boys had built themselves under the direction of the Civil Defence was not big enough to house all of us, so some of us had to sleep under the billiard table in the staff common-room and others under the tables in the dining-room. Though at times I had to go to the shelter, which I hated for it felt like being buried alive, most of the time I arranged things so that I would be among those who stayed in the house. The floor was very hard and uncomfortable, so sometimes in the dead of night I would creep back to my bed and sleep alone in the deserted dormitory. I had to be cunning for if I had been caught I would certainly have received six of the best where it hurts most. I discovered that if I got up just before the morning bell and sneaked down the back stairs and into the wash-house no one would know that I had not spent the night under the billiard table with the rest of the kids provided always that there was not a roll-call or my presence was missed by a 'tell-tale'. Luckily for me neither of these eventualities arose – so most nights I spent in sweet repose in the comfort of my warm bed by the window up in the dormitory. But my guardian angel must have been watching over me, because one night a V 2 rocket came down near-by that might easily have had my number on it. By some extraordinary twist of fate, that was the only night that week that I had *not* been able to get out of spending the night in the shelter. There was a deafening explosion, the shelter shook violently, threatening at any moment to cave in on top of us, the kids began to scream in terror, the master in charge of us, his face chalk-white, ordered us sternly to be silent. Outside fire-engine bells rang and an ARP warden came to see if we were all right; a few of the younger boys still snivelled quietly but otherwise none of us appeared to be any the worse for the shock. 'What fun,' I thought, 'the Jerries have blown up the Home. Now they will have to let me go.' But alas, apart from a gaping hole in the roof, some doors blown off their hinges, all the windows shattered once more and several collapsed ceilings, the sturdy building had survived the explosion remarkably well. When in the morning we ventured back into the house to clear up the mess, I found to my horror that the window next to my bed had been blown in and huge jagged fragments of glass had showered the bed with such force that the mattress was lacerated as though it had suffered the multiple stabbing of a lunatic. Had the rocket come down the night before it is extremely unlikely that I would have lived to tell the tale. But bearing in mind the premise that lightning never strikes in the same place twice (or perhaps after all I was still mentally deranged) I continued to creep off to my bed, or to someone else's not so near the window, whenever I got the chance.

One rule, which actually took the form of a warning, was that we should never pick up any objects lying in the street or anywhere else; for example fountain-pens, cigarette-cases, powder-compacts, ominous-looking boxes and even bars of chocolate, the reason being that it was said that the Germans were showering the countryside with booby-traps disguised as such innocent and highly pick-up-able objects as these. We were deterred not at all, and dived on absolutely everything we saw, but by luck no one was blown to bits, because all of the things that we were fortunate enough to find turned out to be exactly what they purported to be – fountain-pens, cigarette-cases, etc. That is not to say that there were no booby-traps about, we simply didn't find any, that's all.

There was also quite a brisk trade in incendiary-bomb tail-fins, which were collected by the Civil Defence corps as salvage, sent to the armament factories in the North, melted down and made into weapons to be used against the enemy – which seems like poetic justice, as they had been manufactured by Krupps and dropped on the houses of the civilian population in central London. But the ones that did not find their way back to Germany were kept by us as souvenirs or bartered for sweets and cigarettes.

I began to smoke at a very early age, at about twelve years old I should think. My brand was Craven A. To begin with I smoked one a day, half in the morning and half after school in the evening. On the way to school I would sneak into a tobacconist's and bang my money down on the counter and squeak: 'One Craven A please.' At first the man behind the counter was reluctant to serve me, but I would say that it was for my father and he not knowing (and perhaps not caring) that I was telling a lie would hand it over. I became quite a good customer of his, spending the whole of my pocket-money in his shop, which was about fourpence a week. By the time I was thirteen I had an uncontrollable craving for Craven A, and before long for absolutely anything that would burn. My meagre pocket-money soon became insufficient to meet my desire to smoke (for I was now on two and sometimes three cigarettes a day). Often I was reduced to picking up fag-ends from the gutter and rolling them up in cigarette papers.

But I was soon to learn a salutary lesson. There was an old and kindly gentleman who often visited the Home. He was not a member of the staff, just a well-meaning member of the public who felt it his duty to befriend us poor kids without families of our own. Once a week he would obtain permission from the governor to take one or another of us out to tea at his house, or for a walk in the town. He was greatly loved by everyone, for he did not patronize us or make us feel that his kindness was really pity, like so many of the visitors from the outside did. Eventually my turn to go to his house for tea came round, permission was duly granted and off we set. It was a wonderful treat and I enjoyed every minute of his company; he played the piano in his sitting room while I scoffed as many cakes as my insatiable greed would allow. When at last I could eat no more without running the risk of being sick, I sat in an armchair and we talked about every topic under the sun. The old gent was a walking encylopædia, there seemed to be no end to his knowledge. I sat enraptured as he told me about the many parts of the world that he had visited; Tasmania where the sun shone all the year around; Brazil where the Amazon women six feet tall ruled their men with a rod of iron; Alaska where he had once been a fur-trapper; the Kalahari desert where he almost died of thirst and had to fight off a tribe of Fuzzy-wuzzies single-handed; China where he had been a missionary – like Marco Polo he had seen all the mysteries of the Orient. His house was filled with treasures collected from every corner of the globe; perhaps he made the best of many of his stories but I did not care for it was the most unlikely embellishments that I enjoyed the most.

At last it was time for me to leave. I was sad and begged to be allowed to stay longer, but he told me affectionately that he would get into a row with the Governor if I got back too late. Reluctantly I got ready to leave, but made him promise that he would ask me around to his house again in the near future. He smiled upon me benignly and teasingly said that he would have to see about that: 'Please,' I pleaded.

'All right, perhaps next week,' he smiled and gave me a shilling.

'Promise!' I said taking the silver coin and thanking him profusely for it.

'Promise,' he replied.

That night I lay awake for hours thinking of all the things that he had told me. What an exciting life he had had and how I envied him. I think it was quite rare for the same boy to go out with him two weeks running, but sure enough, true to his word, he came for me and off we set for his house once more. All the week I had thought about him and talked about him endlessly to whoever would listen. I seem to remember that I told the matron how much I had enjoyed my outing and perhaps she told the Governor what an improving effect the old gentleman was having upon me, and maybe because of this he permitted me to go again the following week end and the week end after that. Indeed after a few weeks I was allowed to visit my friend whenever I liked, without even having to ask permission. If I did not get back from school in time for tea, the old gentleman would 'phone up to say that I was with him, there would then be no repercussions about my absence. I have no evidence to show what the Governor's motives were in letting me have so much freedom all of a sudden, but the above theory seems to me to be a possibility.

For a time all was well between my new-found friend and me. I went to his house as often as I could and we talked for hours together. I absorbed every word he uttered and learned a great deal; once again it might have looked to the staff at the Home as though I was at long last going to make it. Then one afternoon disaster struck. I popped into the old gentleman's house after school and as usual he was pleased to see me. After welcoming me warmly he asked me if I would care for a glass of iced orange juice, it being a summer's day. I said I would and he left the room to get it. I glanced around, then suddenly I saw them on top of the sideboard, a packet of Craven A. I tried not to look at them, but it was no use, the need for a cigarette was upon me. Furtively I picked up the packet, opened it, took a single cigarette out and slipped it into my pocket, I then put the packet back on the sideboard in exactly the same place as I had found it. The old gentleman then returned carrying a pitcher of orange juice and two glasses, I blandly drank his health (to cover my guilt) and we settled down to our habitual nattering, me asking him questions about things that he had told me the week before, which he answered sometimes very convincingly and other times confusingly. I left early that evening saying that I had to go to a scout meeting, which was an absolute lie. I merely wanted to get the cigarette between my lips and set light to it.

The following afternoon I visited him again and took another from the packet and the next day another, and the next another. Actually I do not think he smoked himself, at least I never saw him, I expect he only bought them to give to his guests. The packet which in the beginning had been almost full was dwindling fast, and I became absolutely petrified of getting caught, but I could not control my compulsion to take one whenever I visited the house. By the end of the second week I had taken about fifteen of my friend's cigarettes and there were now only two or three left. I called on the Saturday afternoon, rang his bell but though I was sure he was in he did not answer. I began to knock on the door softly at first, still he did not answer, and through fear and guilt I suddenly began to hammer on the door with my fist as though my life depended on it, but it availed me nothing but bruised knuckles – he would not open the door to me.

On the Sunday, wearing my scout uniform (I had joined at my friend's instigation several weeks before) we paraded for church, my hat, with its brim reminiscent of a scenic railway, a size too large, resting on my ears. Suddenly a boy whom I knew was also a friend of the old gentleman's sidled up to me and handed me the familiar twenty Craven A packet. 'He told me to give you this,' said the boy. With trembling hands I took the packet and using his back as a shield from the scoutmaster's ever-watchful gaze I slipped it open; inside there were no more cigarettes, just a small piece of paper folded in two. I opened it and read the four words written in block capitals 'YOU FORGOT THE PACKET.' I let the packet fall to the ground and, screwing up the note, stuffed it into my pocket.

'Fall in,' shouted the scoutmaster. 'Attention! By the right quick march!' The pipe band struck up and we marched behind it, my eyes blinded with tears.

For several days after that I lived in terror of being summoned to the Governor's office for a thrashing as punishment for my sneak thievery. But to my astonishment nothing happened. By the end of the week I was in such a state of worry about what my fate was going to be that I took my courage in both hands and went around to the old gentleman's house. With no little trepidation I pressed the door bell and within a few seconds he had opened the door and there we stood facing one another, I shame-faced, he with a stern expression on his face, though he could not entirely blot out the kindly light that perpetually shone in his eyes. He indicated that I should come inside, I followed him into the sitting-room, my head bent in shame.

'Why ever did you do it?' he asked unaccusingly.

'I dunno,' I replied hopelessly.

'The thing is if you do that kind of thing in later life you will end up in the most frightful pickle,' he continued adopting a serious tone, but completely unable to control a slight smile.

'I just did it that's all,' I said. 'I dunno why. I didn't mean to honest I didn't it just sort of 'appened that's all.'

'Well I want you to promise me that you will never do such a thing again,' he said soberly.

'I do, I do honest I do,' I gushed, greatly relieved that it seemed as though I was going to get away with it quite lightly. 'You ain't gonna report me to the Guv'ner are you?' I asked, genuinely frightened.

'No of course not,' smiled the old gentleman. 'Whatever in the world gave you that idea?'

'Well I just thought . . .'

'Look, what happens between my friends and myself has nothing to do with anyone else. As far as I am concerned the matter is now closed and we are still the best of friends. All right?'

'All right,' I muttered still unable to look him in the eye, or believe my luck.

'Good, then let us shake hands then,' he smiled warmly and offered me his hand, which I took in mine and shook as warmly as I could. But his generous nature only served to make my guilt the worse, I had never been forgiven for anything in my entire life and was not easily able to accept it, even from this kindly man who only wished me well. Though I did not cut him off completely I rarely went around to his house after that. How very unfair it was that he should have to suffer for my wrong-doing, for I know that he missed our talks. But he never asked me why my visits had now become so infrequent, he understood why, so it was therefore unnecessary.

My long-awaited opportunity to make friends with the little Spanish boy, whose gymnastic prowess I had so admired on the bars some months before, came about in the most extraordinary way. I had over the weeks tried to make some contact with him, but even though he had now picked up a few phrases of rudimentary English it was still impossible to carry on any sort of conversation, but I am certain that he was aware that I liked him, for he always smiled broadly whenever we ran into each other in the playground or at school and I smiled back as meaningfully as I could – smiles, kisses and punches being international.

As well as the pipe band and Brentford football team the Governor was also interested in boxing. It was more or less compulsory to volunteer to fight, for refusal meant being branded a coward by the rest of the boys and petty victimization by the staff. I think he mistakenly believed these pugilistic contests built up our moral fibre. It was on an occasion when I was matched against a boy with a bright red face, who had high blood pressure, that to my great delight Pedro (not the real name of the Spanish boy) was instructed by the Governor to act as my second. He beamed at me as he rubbed my chest with the rough towel and laced up the boxing gloves at the wrist. I looked back at him sadly and a dark cloud crossed his eyes as he got the message. Both my opponent and I were far from keen to have the bout, but there was no help for it. The bell clanged and Pedro gave me a little encouraging pat on the back as I headed for the centre of the ring, where the other boy waited, his gloved fists dangling aimlessly at his sides – he was absolutely useless in the ring. For a few seconds we faced each other in a rather ridiculous fashion as though wondering what it was we were meant to do. 'Box on!' roared the Governor, 'Show us what you can do!' Seeing that there was absolutely nothing else for it, I brought my fist up and took a blind swipe at the other boy's face; more by luck than from good judgement the blow landed squarely on the end of my luckless adversary's nose, which exploded blood in all directions, drenching us both. A roar of approval went up from the crowd and the bell rang indicating the end of the round, and I thought the end of the match. I ambled back to my corner and slumped onto the stool thoroughly dejected, I absolutely hated what I had done to the other boy, for I only liked to fight when roused on matters of principle or in a blind rage. Pedro on the other hand was delighted with my performance and clapped me on the shoulder as though I was now champion of the world.

Mr Gardener went to the other boy's corner, inspected the damage and declared him fit to continue, 'Seconds away round two!' he bellowed clanging the bell once more. Faintheartedly I shuffled towards the boy and did my utmost to do him no further damage: 'Box him boy, box him!' shouted the Governor. He was an easy target and I thought that if I knocked him to the ground with just one punch they would really have to stop the miserable spectacle. I swung at him several times and though every blow met its mark he wouldn't go down, instead he just bled like a stuck pig, the crowd cheered wildly, I wanted to cry – the bell rang ending the second round and I was sure that the fight would now be stopped. But to my astonishment, after giving the boy a cursory inspection the Governor made us go the final round, making three in all. My blood was now up, not against my pitiful opponent, but against everyone else, the Governor, the cheering boys, the world! When the bell rang I tore out of my corner like a tiger eager for the kill. It flashed through my brain that if I murdered him the Governor would be held responsible, the police would be called and he would be charged and maybe hanged for the crime. I lambasted the boy mercilessly, every blow almost jerking his head from his body, his arms hung limply at his side, he was defeated and utterly unable to defend himself against the onslaught. But still I tore into him, no longer hoping that he would fall to the canvas but instead that he would stay on his feet so that I could kill him. The crowd who had cheered so roisterously throughout the previous rounds suddenly fell silent, perhaps sick with fear and guilt at having made this happen.

'Stop!' yelled the Governor. But I did not hear him. I smashed into the boy's face blindly. 'Stop it, stop it! stop it!' he shouted again, clanging the bell as though it were a fire engine. The boy was now hanging against the ropes crying like a baby: still I went after him, a maniac completely out of control. Suddenly Pedro ran across the ring and pinioned my flaying arms to my side, I tried to break away from him but he clung on like a terrier. Then inexplicably my senses came back to me and I calmed down, not really aware of where I was or what I had done. Gently Pedro took me by the arm and led me back to my corner. As I slumped onto my stool I glanced up at him, my face glistening with sweat, my eyes still wild from the senseless affray. Suddenly a faint smile touched his lips and slowly broadened into a full grin, friendly and warm like the sun of his homeland. I cannot ever remember being closer to a fellow human being than at that precise moment. I smiled back at him: there was now a bond between us, even though no words were spoken.

The Governor came over to my corner and taking me by the wrist led me to the centre of the ring where he raised my arm high in the air and pronounced me the winner. After a slight pause the boys roared their approval and applauded wildly, I waved modestly and returned to my corner a most reluctant hero. For the fight had in the end not been between just the other boy and me but 'me' against all of them and I had inadvertently won. I would now be looked upon with respect, would no longer be given all the rotten jobs to do, the victimization of the staff would also end and all for the wrong reasons. The other boy was carted off to the sickbay and found to be not as mortally wounded as at first had been supposed (certainly from the look of him). True, he had two black eyes, split nose and all the other symptoms that mark a loser. But it was his high blood pressure that had made his defeat look so spectacular.

From that day forward Pedro and I became inseparable, we walked to school together every day and sat next to each other in class, or in the air-raid shelter. We raided orchards, hiding our haul of apples in our gas-mask boxes. As the months passed by his pidgin English began to reach coherence and we were able to talk to each other, as well as instinctively understanding each other's every thought through looks, smiles and gestures. In deeper awareness we would never know each other better than we did already, there was an unexplainable bond between us, chemical and electric. But though words were hardly necessary it was nice to chat together all the same.

Not only was Pedro a marvellous gymnast, he was also a good all-round athlete, he could run fast, swim like a fish, dive like a swallow and jump like a gazelle. He mastered the arts of football and cricket before he had been at the Home a year, before long he was scoring more goals and runs than anyone else on the team, which made him very popular with most of the boys, though there were a few dissenters who loathed him and tried to belittle his talents by shouting 'Here comes the Spanish onion!' whenever they saw him. But Pedro only laughed at their jeers, and as if to add insult to injury he tried even harder to excel at everything that he turned his hand to. He ignored their taunts, for they only stemmed from envy.

I on the other hand was absolutely useless at sports, indeed to have me on your team was a positive handicap. I could swim and play table-tennis, but at both these accomplishments I was never better than passably fair. However on one unfortunate afternoon the school second eleven cricket team were, under duress, compelled to have me on the side, for they were a man short and there was no one else about to make up the number. As a rule I sat in the safety of the pavilion, keeping the score book and no one was less keen than I to take to the field. But there was no help for it, so dressed in white shirt and trousers I ambled out onto the pitch to do fielding, the other side having won the toss and elected to bat first. The captain of the team, a beefy boy with red hair and pimples, ordered me to take the position of long stop, right at the far end of the pitch, indeed on the boundary line where I imagine he thought I could do the least harm. And so play commenced; cricket being a leisurely game I just stood around sunning myself and hoping against hope that I would not have to do any troublesome rushing about after the ball. For a time my luck was in, for the batsmen only hit the ball into areas of the field far away from where I stood, such as the slips and silly-mid-on. After a while I became bored with the inaction of the game and sat down on the newly mown grass, the better to sunbathe. Then suddenly without warning a voice yelled 'Catch!' Thinking the remark was not addressed to me I ignored it: 'Catch!' came the cry again. Opening my eyes I looked up in the sky and saw the cricket ball plummetting through space towards me. In an instant I was on my feet and cupping my hands for the catch; the sun blinded my eyes and I missed it, much to my relief for a cricket ball falling from a great height is liable to be very painful when caught in hands without gloves. It whistled past my ear and landed behind the boundary:

'Six!' shouted the umpire.

'You useless idiot!' the captain shouted at me. Shrugging my shoulders, I searched among the long grass beyond the boundary line and eventually found the ball, which I threw back to the bowler underarm like a girl. 'My God!' shouted the captain roaring across the field in my direction.

'Look, just concentrate on the game will you,' he demanded viciously when he had come abreast of me.

'Sorry,' I replied sheepishly. Throwing his arms in the air in a gesture of hopelessness he headed back to the wicket at a trot and once again took command of the game. It took some time to get the other team out, and the sixth batsman in stubbornly refused to be moved from the wicket and got runs from almost every ball that was tossed down the pitch at him. As the bowlers got tired the umpire (who was also one of the schoolmasters) suggested that *I* should be allowed to bowl an over. Needless to say there was a great deal of opposition to this from the captain of the team and indeed from every other player on the field, excepting perhaps the batsmen who no doubt relished the idea of smashing the ball all over the place. I have to admit that the likelihood of this was very high, for I had never bowled a ball before in my entire life, but the umpire insisted that I should do an over so there I found myself with the ball in my hand standing at the wicket. Walking several yards away from the crease I turned and did my 'run-up', my arm whirling like a windmill sail in a hurricane; when I reached the crease I let the ball go hurling it in the general direction of the batsman at the opposite end. The ball sailed right over his head and many rude remarks were shouted from the fellow-members of my team. The umpire roared with laughter, and gave the ball as a wide. When the ball was returned to me I ran up to the wicket and once again blindly hurled it at the batsman.

''Ow'sat!' bawled every fielder on the pitch as the middle stump at the other end went flying when the ball struck it.

'It was a throw,' said the batsman bitterly.

'It was a legal ball,' said the umpire and, still unable to control his mirth, he gave the boy out. The other members of my team now beginning to enjoy the fun as well, gave a great cheer as I laid the next ball down, which was so wide of the wicket as to be almost in the opposite direction. Eventually my over came to an end amid tumultuous applause, for though I got no further wickets my over had been very cheap on runs, for apart from the second ball the other five had not been anywhere near the wicket and therefore also not within range of the batsman.

Eventually it was our turn to bat, I predictably was last man in, which suited me fine, and indeed I prayed for rain to stop play before my turn came. But it didn't, and so swathed in cricket pads I ventured onto the pitch, bat in hand. When the umpire, with an amused expression still on his face, had lined up my bat with the wicket, I faced the bowler. My heart sank, it was the boy I had bowled out. The first one he chucked down was a bumper, it hit a clod of earth several feet away from me and bounded up, striking me in the chest with great force. I dropped my bat and clutched my breast as though I had been shot, the umpire hurried over to see if I was all right. I gave him a sickly smile and said that I was fine, then picking up my bat I faced the demon bowler once more. The second ball, travelling at the speed of light also bounced up and this time struck me painfully on the biceps of my left arm; I flinched but this time did not drop the bat. Determined not to be defeated I faced the bowler a third time, but now with concentration; I would hit the ball at least once if it killed me. He roared up to the crease like a railway engine and let the ball fly, it scorched down the pitch towards me and I stepped forward to meet it, with all my might and main I took an almighty swipe at it. To my astonishment the leather and wood connected and the ball flew high in the air and away miles over the boundary. The cheer that went up from the pavilion was almost deafening and there were many shouts of: 'Good old Norman!' As calmly as I could I stood at the wicket ready to face the next ball, determined to repeat the performance and compound my success. But alas though I did manage to hit the ball it was only a glancing blow and I was caught by some idiot at silly-mid-on. As I walked back to the pavilion I was well satisfied with my effort and althought we did not ultimately win the match I felt that I had won the game.

.   .   .   .   .

From time to time we were visited by contingents of the US army and air force who were stationed just down the hill in Richmond Park. They were very kind to us and always arrived armed to the teeth with presents of chewing-gum, peanuts, toys, sweets and of course Coca-Cola. After tea they would put on a concert party, each would do a turn, dancing, conjuring, comedy and sketches in which some of them would appear dressed in women's clothes and funny hats; at the end we would all join together in community singing. There was one pilot officer named Tex who was a great favourite with the boys, he was always cheerful and did a fast-talking comedy act. We would roar with laughter at him and after the show he would always come down from the stage and lark about with the kids, distributing sweets and telling jokes. Pedro took a great fancy to his peaked cap, which had a huge bronze eagle on it and the letters USAAF. Whenever Tex came to see us he would let Pedro wear it until it was time for them to go. Pedro was always reluctant to give it up and sometimes made a hell of a fuss about it.

'Come on kiddo gimme my hat,' Tex would laugh. 'I'll be back next Saturday then you can wear it all day.' Thus reassured Pedro would hand it over, he was more attached to the hat than Tex was himself. I am not sure which aerodrome they took off from but I know that they went on German bombing raids almost every day and a good many of them were shot down, but they never talked to us about that and we never asked them. One day Tex told Pedro that he was going to be transferred elsewhere. My little Spanish friend was extremely upset and seemed near to tears, but he put a brave face on the inevitable and handed the hat over with as much of a smile as he could muster. Later in the evening a squadron of bombers flew low over the Home (as they so often did), we stood gawping up at them and waved till our arms hurt, then suddenly something fluttered out of one of the windows of the leading bomber, it drifted to earth landing in the kitchen garden, there was a wild stampede as some fifty boys trampled over one another to find out what it was; as they entered the kitchen garden there hanging from an apple-tree was Tex's hat, tucked inside it there was a note which read 'To Pedro with love from Tex'. In spite of this the Governor would not let him keep it, it was instead put in a glass case and kept in the front hall. I do not think that Pedro minded that he was not allowed to wear it, he seemed perfectly happy in the knowledge that he could look at it whenever he wanted to.

The Heavyweight Champion of the World, Joe Louis, was also stationed at Richmond Park, and though he did not come to the Home he did invite us to come and watch him have an exhibition bout. Most of the boys were very excited about it, but not I, for I had lost my taste for the noble art of self-defence. Joe Louis often gave these exhibitions bouts to raise money for charity, which is no doubt why the American Government let him off his income tax in the end.

At school I remained the dunce of my class. I simply could not absorb the lessons; upon reflection this could not entirely be blamed on the war for most of the other pupils seemed to make fair enough progress, and a good many of them were from the Home. I just couldn't seem to get down to it, I knew that I could learn if I tried but something was blocking me mentally. I cannot even today say what exactly it was for in some aspects I am the same now as I was then. Perhaps, as the psychologists say, our most formative years are the ones that few of us remember – one to four. Certainly there was a malignant gremlin in my brain in those days, whose sole purpose seemed to be to mess me up at every turn. On the surface it must have seemed to those in authority over me that I was anti-social and impervious to education.

In other words an avowed troublemaker. But on the other hand I was never a ring-leader, indeed except for my friendship with Pedro I kept myself more or less to myself. I hardly ever joined anything, though as mentioned earlier I did join the scouts, but was soon chucked out for I was never 'prepared' and as a result did not pass my 'Tenderfoot' examination. Indeed I did not come anywhere near passing it. I hated granny and reef knots, could not abide sleeping in tents, loathed singing round the old camp fire; 'Underneath the spreading chestnut tree' was particularly nauseous to me, I thought that rubbing two sticks together in order to make fire was an utterly futile way to pass the time and five-mile hikes with heavy haversacks strapped to one's back seemed to me to be the ultimate in masochism. I was delighted when they let me go. Strangely enough my friend Pedro revelled in this kind of activity, which irritated me greatly because it deprived me of his company for much of the time, doing good deeds to old ladies, tying knots in bits of rope and one thing and another. Predictably he soon became a patrol leader and I saw him even less.

But my liking for nature study, which I had first taken to at the Bedford Home, stayed with me and indeed does to this very day. I would ramble alone in the woods near by, never with permission for they were very strictly out of bounds, unless we were accompanied by a member of the staff. But I hated organized walks and crept off on my own whenever the opportunity arose of doing so without being found out. I collected hazel nuts and crab-apples and would have picked bluebells as well if it had not been for the certainty of being called a sissy by the rest of the boys, if they ever found out. For hours I would lie on my back in the bracken listening to the song-birds and watching the squirrels leap from branch to branch like aerial artistes; now and then a rabbit would hop by, unafraid of my presence because he was unaware of it.

I lay still as a log, fearing almost to breathe lest I should disturb the tranquillity that surrounded me. Now and then I would see a fox stalking through the undergrowth on the scent of some unsuspecting prey, but the rarest and greatest treat was to see a deer, and best of all a deer accompanied by a noble stag. I would become like stone when I saw them approaching, for I knew that the slightest movement – the snapping of a twig, the rustle of bracken – would startle them and put them on their guard. They would browse on the spring leaves and shoots of the trees, sometimes the stag would have a mock battle with an invisible adversary, lowering his antlers and pawing the ground before making a short little charge, or he would stand close to his doe as though protecting her from unknown dangers, sharpening his antlers on the bark of the nearest tree-trunk the while. There were many deer in Richmond Park, of which the wood was part. But they mostly kept to the open spaces, wandering about in small herds for safety. They were under Royal protection, but a flying-bomb is no respecter of Royal Proclamations. As I wandered alone in the wood I often thought of Hilda May and Miss Love, for I missed them both greatly. I wondered if Hilda May still occupied the hollow oak and if she had found someone new to share it with. I also missed the meadow and the rural atmosphere of Bedford. Would I go and see them all again when I grew up? (I never did.)

One night Pedro and I were playing draughts in the air-raid shelter when quietly he began to sing a gay Spanish song:

> De la sierra morena,
> Cielito lindo,
> Vienen bajando,
> Un par ojitos negros,
> Cielito lindo, de contrabando.

> Ay, ay, ay, ay.
> Canta y no llores,
> Porque cantando se alegran,
> Cielito lindo, los corazones.

I asked him what it meant, but apart from telling me it was Mexican his English was not good enough to translate it. I told him that I wanted to learn it whether I knew what the words meant or not. He grinned and sang it again and again over and over until at last I had more or less learned it parrot-fashion. So pleased was I with this small achievement that after singing it with him a couple of hundred times I offered to give a rendering of it solo, which to my astonishment I did with the greatest *éclat*. Pedro clapped his hands gleefully to the rhythm and when I finished shouted 'Bravo, bravo compadre!' So naturally I had to sing it again for an encore, but stumbled over the first verse a little, Pedro just laughed and came to my aid, filling in the words that I had missed or had difficulty in pronouncing. It is a song I have remembered all my life, though my Spanish accent leaves a very great deal to be desired. A rough translation of it into English goes something like:

> From the black mountain,
> a pair of black eyes,
> are being smuggled down.
>
> Ay, ay, ay, ay.
> Sing and don't cry,
> Because singing makes
> The heart happy.

How enigmatic can you get? Still, in Spanish it sounds marvellous. Pedro knew a good many more songs and though I picked one or two of them up, I soon forgot them. Only *Cielito Lindo* has stayed with me. In exchange I taught him:

The grand old Duke of York,
He had ten thousand men,
He marched them up to the top of the hill.
And he marched them down again.
And when they were up they were up,
And when they were down they were down.
And when they were only half-way up,
They were neither up nor down.

I realize of course that it was hardly a fair barter, but unfortunately I had nothing else to offer, except for a few prayers and songs of praise that I would not have the temerity to offer to my worse enemy, let alone best friend. However Pedro seemed perfectly happy with the idiotic rhyme and repeated it over and over in the same way as I had his song, until eventually he was word-perfect. I do hope that he hasn't had the misfortune to remember it all of his life.

The outside school that we went to was divided into two halves, one half for the boys and the other for girls, a wall separating the two playgrounds like an iron curtain. It was strictly forbidden for us to enter the girls' playground on any pretext whatever. If for instance someone kicked a football over the wall, they had to wait till the girls threw it back, or else ask a master to go and fetch it. Most of the time this rule was strictly adhered to, and we satisfied our curiosity about the opposite sex by gawping at them through the gate when they were playing netball. Now and then an intrepid fellow might venture into the forbidden territory, but within seconds he would be chased out again by a horde of angry girls brandishing hockey-sticks. One day a luckless interloper had the great misfortune to be captured by the girls and dragged off into one of the classrooms in their half of the building. He kicked, screamed and howled but it did him not the slightest bit of good, they overpowered him and he was done for. From inside the classroom his howling could still be heard, we stared, our eyes agog, wondering what on earth they could be doing to him, then suddenly he came belting out of the door and across the playground, clutching his trousers at the waist. He reached the gate leading to our side within a second, jerked it open and leapt to safety. The girls then emerged on their side laughing and giggling.

'What on earth did they do to you?' said one of the boys, asking the question that was in all of our minds.

'They, they, they. . . .' he replied his voice choked with sobs.

'THEY WHAT??' we yelled in unison.

'They rubbed boot polish on me.'

'WHERE?' we shouted again.

'On my thing.'

'They *never*,' said someone in disbelief.

'They did, look.' He unbuttoned his trousers and showed us. Sure enough his little dick and bottom had been smeared with Cherry Blossom; we were aghast and for a time gazed in silence at his negro bottom half. After that no one had the courage to venture into the girls' half. There was some talk about making reprisals but they soon died down, for the truth of the matter was that we were too scared to do anything. Most of the boys were well able to take care of themselves in a punch-up on fairly matched terms, but against a horde of wild schoolgirls, never – we would have rather have faced the might of the entire Axis forces. It is really quite astonishing how much ruder girls can be than boys at times.

On 30th April 1943 the Governor of the Kingston Home sent the following report on my progress to the Chief Superintendent at head office:

*Behaviour:* F/G. *Progress at school:* Fair. *Habits:* Clean.

*Relatives who keep in touch:* No.

(There followed several comments.) A peculiar boy mentally. Making little progress. Very sullen.

There is not really very much I can add to that, except perhaps 'And the same to you.' The biggest trouble between me and them was that they didn't understand me and I didn't understand them. But that is really only the half of it, for if, say, I had been better at my lessons or perhaps good at sports they would have been well pleased with me. My problem with hating them however was an entirely mental thing, deep to the very roots of my being. They had not an ounce of love and affection for any of us; 'Obey the rules or take the consequences' was their motto. If a boy excelled at the Home it could only mean that he had knuckled under and lost his identity. There was however one master whom I seemed to get along with quite well; he was a harsh man but somehow was fairer than the others, which only means that he never clumped me around the ear when I had done nothing to deserve it. One year at Christmas-time I made a picture calendar at school and decided to give it to that master as a present. On Christmas Eve I stole into his room and laid it neatly on his pillow, together with a small greetings card which I had also made. The following morning as we assembled on church parade for the Christmas service, he took me aside and rather irritably asked me why I had put the calendar on his bed.

'It's a present sir,' I replied, 'for Christmas sir.'

'Well you shouldn't have done it,' he said gruffly, though without anger.

'It was a pleasure sir,' said I.

'I just don't like to be obligated to any of you boys, that's all,' he said, the Christmas spirit now visibly deserting him.

'I didn't mean no 'arm sir,' beginning to quake at the knees.

'I don't want you to think that you are going to get any special treatment just because you have given me a present, that's all,' he replied.

'No sir, I weren't thinking of that sir.'

'That's all right then,' he snapped, taking a shilling from his pocket and pressing it into my palm. 'Now I have given you a present and we are even, all right?'

'Yes sir,' I replied, beginning to feel absolutely rotten and wishing to God that I had not bothered to make the effort. But I suppose as I was by no means renowned for giving presents to members of the staff, he had good reason for thinking that I had some sort of ulterior motive. But I wish he had not, for I had no other reason in giving him the calendar than that it was Christmas. How I wished I *had* as we marched down the hill to church.

The war was now being fought with concentrated fury in North Africa. It was costing the Germans dearly, which turned out to be to our advantage at home, in more ways than one, for it meant that the Luftwaffe had to give up their efforts to blow the British Isles off the face of the earth (enemy air power now being needed to destroy ships and tanks instead of people's houses). Raids on London became fewer and fewer until eventually they became a rarity.

Instead of invading us a couple of years earlier, when they would have almost certainly been able to over-run the country with little resistance within a couple of weeks, Hitler in his stupidity went off in the opposite direction and attacked Russia, which many pundits say cost him the war. On the radio we now listened to encouraging dispatches from the front – Monty's 'Desert Campaign' was on everyone's lips from morning till night and Vera Lynn sang: 'Underneath the lamplight by the barracks gate. . . .' until I am certain she was blue in the face. There was in the air an atmosphere of euphoria as the greatly outnumbered 8th Army routed Rommel's crack Panzer Divisions until at last they were utterly vanquished. It seemed as though the tide had turned at last, indeed it now appeared as though we would ultimately win the war. But then of course the British are renowned for their ability to lose every battle except the last one.

Though we still carried our gas masks with us wherever we went, there seemed now to be little point in it. For not a whiff of it was dropped throughout the whole of the war, and there now seemed to be little chance that it ever would be. I understand from reliable sources that this was because, if the Germans had dropped any on us, we would have dropped ten times as much of it on them. And due to the air currents around the British Isles the gas would have soon dispersed, while in Germany the effects of gas would have been disastrous. In that inland country the air currents are far less turbulent, the gas would therefore have taken far longer to disperse. In the early days we used to have gas-mask inspection at least once a week, but now they had become a rarity. I found my gas-mask box a very good receptacle for smuggling contraband articles in and out of the Home. I would hide my gas mask under my pillow and fill the box with such things as margarine, sugar and cheese, all of which I pinched from the kitchen. Food rationing was at its peak, and such things fetched a good price from the outside boys at the school, who took them home to their mothers – without any questions being asked. I ran a thriving business, indeed for a time I was king of the black-marketeers and had a capital of about fourteen or fifteen shillings, enough cigarette money to last me several weeks. Though I was never caught I gave it up after a while, perhaps through guilty conscience, or more likely not wanting to tempt providence too far. It is a pity that the business acumen that I had in those days did not stay with me in later life.

My anti-social tendencies and loathing of authority would sometimes reach malicious proportions. I remember on one occasion I was coming home from school with Pedro and a group of other boys, we were kicking an old tin can along the street and were rather boisterous as the boys barged each other violently off the pavement into the path of oncoming traffic in order to get a boot at the tin can. All games in those days were needle matches no matter how trivial. An elderly copper approached us as we rounded a corner and told us (in an officious tone of voice) to pack it up, before someone was injured. For some reason this made me angry, but I managed to contain myself and continued along the street without saying a word. Then when the old copper had turned his back I picked up the old tin can and hurled it at him, hitting him in the small of the back; he whirled around, his face scarlet and his eyes blazing with rage. 'Who threw that?' he demanded. 'Come on, out with it.' No one moved or said a word.

'I know you come from the Home,' he roared. 'If whoever threw the tin does not own up, I will report the lot of you to the Governor.

Still we remained silent, then surreptitiously I sidled up behind a little inoffensive boy called Ginger and unnoticed by anyone pointed at the back of his head several times. I caught the copper's eye and mouthed: 'He did it, he did it.' I continued to jab my finger at the back of poor old Ginger's head. The copper read my lips in a second and without saying a word, took several paces forward and gave the unsuspecting Ginger a stinging clip around the ear with his white gloves.

'What's that for?' yelped Ginger in astonishment. 'I didn't do nothing.'

'You didn't eh?' roared the copper whacking him again this time around the other ear. 'Just you get along home before you find yourself in real trouble.' With that we hurried away, the copper watching us till we were out of sight. I tried desperately hard to keep a straight face but could not contain myself especially when Ginger began to complain bitterly about the injustice of it all. Suddenly I roared with laughter and was soon joined by the rest of the boys (laughter being contagious) but Ginger never did see the joke. It is perhaps of interest to note that in those days it was rare that a policeman would arrest a young boy for such minor infractions of the law – a right-hander being far swifter justice. Today of course it is a different matter, a boy in identical circumstances would very likely be hauled up in front of the juvenile court and sent to a remand home or detention centre.

At the school almost all the teachers were women. The one who took my class was a tremendous dragon and fantastic tyrant, I feared and hated her from the first moment that I clapped eyes on her. She was very tall – over six foot I shouldn't wonder. She had wild black hair as coarse as wirewool – it looked as though it had never seen a hair-brush. On her upper lip there was a moustache that would have certainly put a fledgling Spitfire pilot to shame, her nose was hawk-like and her eyes black and piercing. Just the look of her chilled me to the marrow, she was a spinster and no doubt took a perverse delight in working her frustrations out on us. Her speciality was the unexpected rap over the knuckles with a foot rule. She would stalk stealthily along the rows of desks, then suddenly 'Wham!' down would come the ruler on the knuckles of some unsuspecting boy, reading a comic under his desk instead of studying his twelve times table. One day she caught me doing something or other under the desk (I can't remember what). Silently she crept up behind me and 'Wham!' down came the ruler on the back of my hand. I let out a squawk loud enough to wake the dead – more I think from fright than from pain.

'You bloody bugger!' I yelled (a favourite oath of mine in those days when roused).

'What did you say?' she asked in horror, her face turning as white as a sheet.

'You heard,' I shouted and without more ado hurled my slate at her (they were still in use then for arithmetic). It missed her by a yard but she screamed at the top of her voice: 'Leave the room this instant and go to the headmaster's office!' I got to my feet and shuffled slowly towards the door. 'You will never have a day's good luck as long as you live,' she cackled as I reached for the door knob. She delivered the curse with such venom that I slithered the rest of the way out of the room like a cringing cur. Perhaps she *was* a witch, for it was many years before I had even a modicum of good luck, but then I hadn't had a great deal of it prior to the incident either.

On the first Saturday in every month there was a film show in the gym, folding chairs were set out in rows and there we would sit for an hour or two transported by the antics of Eddie Cantor and Charlie Chaplin and terrorized by the violence of James Cagney and George Raft. If one had been badly behaved near to the time that a film was due to be shown, the punishment was invariably being banned from seeing it. Towards the end of each month my behaviour would inexplicably become exemplary, I would have preferred to have six strokes of the cane across my bare buttocks than be stopped from seeing the film, no matter how bad it was – and most of them were dreadful. Actually, I was prevented from attending the film show once or twice and was instead ordered to stay in the dormitory, but I discovered that if I crept through the back door of the gym behind the screen I could hide in a dark corner and watch the film backwards, then when the picture came to an end I would hastily creep out again and belt back to the dormitory hell for leather and leap into bed. Then the other boys would troop in and describe the movie to me in every detail; many of their descriptions were totally inaccurate but I refrained from correcting them, for to have done so would have been to give myself away, thereby running the grave risk of being snitched on by some goody-goody jealous of my disobedience. Human nature is indeed an extraordinary thing; children, and many grown-ups too, for that matter, dearly love to see people punished (so long as it is not them). It's a kind of one-upmanship, for some ridiculous reason great store is set on being able to take one's punishment like a man!

There were three types of films that I was absolutely mad about – swashbuckling epics starring Errol Flynn, Douglas Fairbanks, Jr., and Tyrone Power, gangster films with Bogart, Cagney, Kirk Douglas and Alan Ladd and last but by no means least Johnny Weissmuller *Tarzan* films. I also quite enjoyed the Marx brothers as light relief. I absolutely loathed musicals and mushy love stories. My favourite actresses were Greta ('I vant to be alone') Garbo, Lana Turner, Joan Crawford, Jane Russell and Paulette Goddard. For many years I had a fantasy about Loretta Young that amounted almost to an obsession and I fell in love and mooned over Madeleine Carroll for many months after seeing her performance in *The Thirty-Nine Steps*. But then I always did have impeccable taste. Though many of the pictures that we saw were home-grown, there was not a solitary English actor or actress that I cared for, though I did have a 'thing' about Patricia Roc once.

There was one gangster film, the end of which I remember vividly. The villain of the piece, after shooting his way out of many tight situations, was chased by the police to the very pinnacle of the Statue of Liberty where he crouched, his gun now empty, waiting to be taken. The heroic police lieutenant clambered up after him, and I sat riveted to my seat thinking that at any minute he would fall to his death as the wind whistled around his ears. Eventually he reached the villain and grabbed hold of the sleeve of his jacket; 'Okay buster the jig's up,' said the copper.

'You ain't takin' me alive,' quoth the villain and tried to kick the copper over the edge, but the good lieutenant clung onto the Statue of Liberty with one hand whilst keeping a firm grip on the 'wrongo's' jacket with the other. Suddenly the baddy lost his balance and toppled off the ledge and for several minutes dangled in mid-air, the policeman still grittily hanging onto his sleeve, which had now become the gangster's only thread between life and death. Slowly the seam began to split at the arm-pit, and a close-up showed an expression of terror on the hood's face. The tear became worse, but still the copper clung on doggedly, the veins at his temple pulsating; at last the cloth rent in two and the arm parted company with the sleeve. As the luckless law-breaker plummeted to his death he let out a piercing cry: 'My sleeeeeeeeeeeeeeeeeeeeeeeeeeeeeeeeeeeeeeeeeeeve !!!!!!' getting fainter and ever fainter till he hit the ground with a sickening thud. The copper remained on the ledge, the villain's sleeve still clutched in his fist, waving about like a flag in the wind. It was a salutary lesson to us all and for many weeks after we went around yelling:
'My sleeeeeeeeeeeeeeeeeeeeeeeeeeeeeeeeeeeeeeeeeeeve !!!!!!' at the tops of our voices all over the place.

Now and then a play was produced by one of the masters, usually at Christmas but at other times as well such as Easter or the Summer holidays. The most memorable was *The Monkey's Paw*. It was also the most chilling and in a way had great truth in it, the main plot being that when you wish for something things can go wrong even if the wish is granted. How often I have wished myself out of one mess and another only to find myself in a worse plight than I was in the first place – the cure for ailments very often being more painful than the diseases.

On dried potatoes, powdered egg, fried Spam, porridge and bread smeared with margarine, we thrived. My growth which in my younger days was slow now got a move on, and by the time I was thirteen I had become a strapping great lad, with an expression on my face that looked as though it should have been on a police WANTED poster. Indeed although I always seemed to be able to retain my sense of humour no matter what, I was growing into a thoroughly anti-social member of society. I was utterly unable to hide my resentment of the staff at the Home and the teachers at the school. Educationally I was improving slightly but progress was slow, more I think from idleness than lack of intelligence. I saw no point in stupid classes anyway and reading books was an utter waste of time. I worked very hard at dodging all the classes I could and therefore learned very little.

On 15th November 1943 my mother wrote the following letter to the head office at Stepney:

Dear Sir,
   I am writing in asking if I could have my Son John Norman Home or as he got to stay untill the War is over been as he is on National Importance work I expect he feels it now as hes 2 Brothers are at home or if not could he come home for Xmas on a Holiday for a week or tow if you would write & let me know I should be very gratefull.

I am your faithful.

                                        Mrs Norman.

And that since the severing of my umbilical cord is the only contact I have had with the lady either directly or indirectly. Whether this letter was a belated act of motherly love, or whether she wanted me home because I was approaching school-leaving age (and could go to work), I will never know. She was at the time living in Birmingham where a Barnardo's inquiry officer visited her and recommended to the General Superintendent that I should spend the following Christmas with her. Leave was granted. But I think she must have got cold feet at the last minute, for I did not go, nor have I heard a word from her since, or the two aforementioned brothers.

Two things occur to me about this letter apart from its idiocy. Firstly if she was still 'separated from her husband' as stated in my dossier (which seems highly likely as the letter is signed with her maiden name with an erroneous Mrs added), then the second of my half-brothers has a different father from the first. Secondly it seems hard to believe that she had ever been 'a secretary at some works' for it is self-evident that she was ill-equipped for such a post. But then, as was pointed out to me by a Barnardo's representative, they have to take the information given to them about a boy or girl before admission on its face value and hope that it is somewhere near the truth. A final point worth mentioning perhaps is that the letter was handwritten: the mistakes (spelling, grammar, etc.) could not therefore have been due to anything other than illiteracy.

That Christmas a present arrived from her – it was a toy aerodrome and several lead aircraft – there was no letter nor a card.

Having retired from the black market, Pedro and I went into the less dangerous business of collecting cigarette-cards and marbles. Actually Pedro had not had anything to do with my previous illicit trading, mainly because I had not invited him to join me, but also because his English was not good enough to conduct it safely. But with cigarette-cards and marbles little talk was necessary. Though we did acquire a good many through bartering with the other boys, for such things as incendiary-bomb fins, our main source was through a mild form of gambling. Cigarette-cards would be flicked up against the wall and the first to cover one card with another picked up the lot, Pedro was an absolute whiz at this game, whilst I on the other hand was rather better at the game of marbles, indeed after many months' practice my aim became absolutely deadly – I could hit my opponent's alley at a distance of some ten to twelve feet nine times out of ten without the slightest difficulty. Within a comparatively short time we became cigarette-card and marble millionaires and the rest of the boys were reluctant to play with us. I became a sort of cigarette-card junky and would not rest until I had completed every set on the market – mostly there were fifty to a set. They covered many fields, film stars, footballers, cars, aeroplanes, trains and flags. My favourites were cars and trains, and I would willingly swop Stanley Matthews for the Flying Scotsman or Clapham and Dwyer, Arthur Askey, Max Miller and Cicely Courtneidge for a single copy of a Citroën if I needed it to complete the set of cars.

It is really quite extraordinary to me that Pedro and I managed to stay friends at all, for he was now absolutely besotted with sport and devoted almost the whole of his spare time to it. Even if there was not a cricket or football match on at the school he would organize an impromptu game picking scratch sides from the other boys wishing to play, the teams being chosen 'Enie-meenie-miney-mo' fashion, so that all the good players did not get on one side and the bad on the other. If the game was to be football, coats would be laid out on the ground to act as goal-posts, the boys would then barge each other about as they kicked the stupid leather bag of wind first in one direction and then the other. If it was to be cricket, stumps and bails would be drawn on the wall with chalk and play would commence. How bored I was by the whole thing! I saw absolutely no sense in it whatever. I despised sport and those who played it, but not half as much as they despised me.

On occasions I would stand on the side-lines and shout sarcastic remarks at the players, which very often reached the lengths of being downright abusive: 'Hoorah for old butter-fingers!!' I would yell when some boy had missed a catch, 'You wonna getcha eyes tested!' when another had missed an open goal. Pedro would glance at me reproachfully, but undeterred I would continue the barrage till hoarse or bored or both. I would then slink off by myself till tea-time or bed-time even, for very often these games would go on until the light had faded.

From the first day that I arrived at the Kingston Home I had been fascinated by the band, and as mentioned earlier I had requested to join it on several occasions but was always rejected out of hand. I had now accepted the fact that I would never be in it, and as a reprisal against myself and the staff I steadfastly took no interest in any other activity. How I envied the virtuosity of the musicians. Often I would creep into the gym during band practice but was always turfed out by the bandmaster; I would then sit outside by the window and listen to the skirl of the pipes for half an hour or more before ambling away disconsolately.

On Sundays the pipers led the church parade, and how magnificent they looked in their Highland kilts with sporrans dangling, their Harris tweed jackets and tooled leather brogues. The drum major strode at their head, his gilt and silver mace glinting in the sunshine as he twirled it in the air. How proud and arrogant he looked as he strutted along like a vainglorious peacock, the kettle drums rattling, the bass drum thumping and the pipes wailing like scalded cats behind him. How I longed to be in his place – I had about as much chance of that as of being struck by lightning.

In the summer the band would go on tour, travelling up and down the country giving concerts, thereby raising much-needed money for the Homes. Sometimes they were away for as long as a fortnight and what tales they would have to tell upon their return. We listened agog as they told us of the wonders of the outside world. Until then I had not even heard of such places as Chesterfield, Newhaven, Huntingdon and Aylesbury. Once they even went across the border into Scotland to take part in the Edinburgh Festival. One of the bandboys even told me that he kissed a girl in Basingstoke but I didn't believe him. How jealous I was of their exploits. I became even more sullen and resentful, if that were possible.

Very often after school we would help the volunteer potato-pickers who worked on utilized stretches of waste land, land which had been barren but now with the use of a little fertilizer had become valuable agricultural soil. We worked until dusk and from a distance our shadowy figures must have looked eerie – like a Van Gogh charcoal sketch. It was man's work, but had to be done for the food shortage was getting no better and every ounce had to be conserved. We built huge potato-clamps from straw, so that the crop would be protected from the hard winter's frost: they looked like giants' graves, as tall as two men and as long as a cricket pitch. I did not mind the work, for I was often able to cadge a smoke from one of the land girls or farm labourers. Now and then there were accidents, one boy jammed a fork through his foot instead of into the ground and another strained himself through rather over-enthusiastically trying to hump a hundredweight sack of spuds onto the back of the farm wagon by himself. But it was all for the war effort and worse things were happening to the Tommies in the front line, we were told.

I was aware that men and women were being killed every day, but not having any family of my own the real horror of the war was never clear to me. I would never be told that a loved one of mine had been killed for I had no loved ones, my house could not be bombed for I did not have one. I lived in limbo, not really caring about anyone and nobody caring about me. I had my friend Pedro but like all childhood relationships it lacked substance, we could at any time have fallen out over the smallest thing and become arch-enemies. Petty squabbles over trivial matters were daily ocurrences at the Home and fist-fights were as common as dirt.

One day at Bible class the teacher said that the vicar had asked her to collect the names of anyone who wished to become Confirmed Christians. Several of the children put their names down and I added my name to the list. The devil only knows why for I was already a Confirmed Atheist! We were told that it was necessary for us to attend confirmation classes, where we would be taught the Catechism and that we would be required to repeat the vows of our godparents. This immediately presented me with a problem for I had not the slightest idea who my godmothers or godfathers might be or indeed if I had ever had any at all. I mentioned my dilemma to the vicar at the first of the classes and he said that it did not matter, I could repeat the vows anyway and take a chance on whether I had any godparents or not. And so our tuition began with the Creed.

'I believe in God the Father Almighty, Maker of heaven and earth: And in Jesus Christ his only son our Lord, Who was conceived by the Holy Ghost, Born of the Virgin Mary, Suffered under Pontius Pilate, Was crucified, dead and buried. He descended into hell. The third day he rose again from the dead. He ascended into heaven. And sitteth at the right hand of God the Father Almighty; From thence he shall come to judge the quick and the dead.

'I believe in the Holy Ghost: The holy Catholic Church: The Communion of Saints: The Forgiveness of sins: The Resurrection of the body: And the Life everlasting. Amen.'

I believed none of it and yet learned it off by heart and remember it to this day. I also learned by heart the Ten Commandments: 'Though shalt not have any other God, make any graven images, take the Lord's name in vain, work on Sundays; Thou shalt honour thy father and mother, do no murder, not commit adultery, not steal, bear false witness or covet other people's property.' Of the ten, I have managed to get through my life so far without killing anyone or making any graven images, the parental one does not apply to me and the rest I have broken times without number, some more than others but quite a respectable score just the same. On the jolly day of judgement (I honestly do not believe there will be such a thing) my maker and I will have much to talk about. To me religion is pure hocus-pocus, but that is not the same as saying that many of the doctrines do not make sense, for certainly they do. Who would not agree that people should not kill each other, steal from each other, hate each other and fight with each other? And yet all of these things happen daily very often in the name of God. It is the ritual, inconsistencies and the stupid threat of hell-fire and damnation that make me an agnostic. Life certainly is hell, but death is merely a merciful release, and that is all there is to it, the idea that there can be a life hereafter is to me plain impossible. If religion can make bad people good and good people better then I am not against it, but the idea of grovelling to some invisible force is entirely alien to my nature, therefore to do so would be to go against my instincts which could hardly be uplifting for my soul. If one is honest to oneself and tolerant of others, there is little more that can be asked of a frail human being.

The day of my Confirmation arrived and the Bishop in all his regalia arrived at the church to do the 'laying on of hands.' The children, spruced up in their Sunday clothes, filed into the pews and whispered quietly whilst they waited for the service to begin. The Bishop entered, followed by the choir, and all fell silent. In solemn tone he then began the ritual: 'Do ye here, in the presence of God, and this congregation, renew the solemn promise and vow that was made in your name at your Baptism. . . .' He rambled on and when he had done we replied: 'I do.'

BISHOP: 'Our help is in the Name of the Lord.'
ANSWER: 'Who hath made heaven and earth.'
BISHOP: 'Blessed be the name of the Lord.'
ANSWER: 'Henceforth, world without end.'
BISHOP: 'Lord, hear our prayers.'
ANSWER: 'And let our cry come unto thee.'
BISHOP: 'Let us pray.'

We all knelt down and the Bishop recited a long prayer beseeching the Lord to give us the strength to keep the vows we were taking. When he had finished we rose to our feet and pushing and shoving formed an orderly queue in the aisle facing the altar. The Bishop sat on a throne slightly to one side of it and blessed each child as they stepped forward and knelt before him. The whole thing was somewhat reminiscent of a conveyor-belt, as one after the other they received the 'laying on of hands' and a mumbled prayer. Eventually it was my turn. Stepping forward I fell to my knees on the hassock in front of the venerable cleric, as though my soul was tormented with the sins of the entire world. But in truth all that had happened was that I had got carried away with the mood of the moment. The Bishop raised his bejewelled hand, placed it upon my head and in a barely audible tone mumbled: 'Defend O Lord, this thy Child with thy heavenly grace, that he may continue thine for ever; and daily increase in thy holy Spirit more and more, until he come unto thy everlasting kingdom. Amen.'

Having so said he took his hand from my head and I lurched to my feet and blindly stumbled away, almost colliding with the next in line. When the last had knelt before the Bishop we sang Hymn 733 (*Hymns Ancient and Modern*):

> Once pledged by the Cross,
> As Children of God,
> To tread in the steps
> Your Captain has trod,
> Now seal'd by the SPIRIT
> Of wisdom and Might,
> Go forward, Christ's soldiers,
> Go forward and fight!

Then after being blessed once more we repaired to the vicarage for a well-earned high tea. Now that I had been confirmed, I could if I wished go to the Holy Communion service on Sunday mornings. I had been told that anyone attending the service was given bread and wine. I could hardly wait. But it turned out to be very disappointing, for the bread was merely a thin wafer and the vicar pulled the chalice away from my lips, without giving me a chance to taste its contents. At the end of the service I was greatly irritated as I watched him gulp the dregs himself, when not a soupçon had I had. I only went the one time.

During the whole of my childhood God the Father, God the Son and God the Holy Ghost were rammed down my throat, like over-sold pop stars. It is little wonder that they got up my nostrils, and that I rejected them the moment that I gave religion any serious thought. It was rather like someone working in a sweet factory, they soon become sick of chocolate. My views on religion are of course by no means unique, but perhaps worth mentioning all the same. I understand that Barnardo's consider they have been successful with children if, after they leave their care they lead 'Christian, sober and industrious lives.' It must follow therefore that they think me a very great failure indeed.

The most sought-after employment in the institution was that of a 'bread-spreader' and by some freak of extraordinary circumstance I was elevated to this plum position for a whole month. The job entailed rushing home from school before the other boys and cutting and spreading the bread for tea. Each boy was rationed to two slices of bread and margarine and a mug of tea. On Sundays there was watery jam, on other days there was cheese or beetroot and on some days there was nothing extra. The advantage of being a 'bread spreader' was that you could ram great hunks of bread and marge down your throat when the master supervising the work was not looking. One could also cut huge slices for oneself and friends. The master in charge of the operation was usually the one to whom I gave the Christmas calendar. Being a reasonably fair man, he did not mind the 'bread-spreaders' treating themselves to huge doorsteps of bread spread with margarine a quarter of an inch thick, provided they did their job of cutting and spreading without mishap. If by accident one of the boys was a slice short on his plate when he came in for tea, the master would confiscate an outsized slice from one of the 'bread-spreaders'. So great care was always taken that there were no slip-ups.

On the days there was cheese, I would stuff myself so full of it before tea that when I sat down to the meal I could not eat a thing. But food was of immense value. For a slice of bread I could get someone to make my bed for a week and for two they would clean my boots and polish the floor around my bed as well.

One day the boy on the manual bread-slicer was twirling the handle at a fantastically rapid rate, the slices tumbled off the end like playing-cards and the half-dozen spreaders applied margarine to them with such speed one would have thought that eating bread was going out of style. Suddenly the last slice of one of the huge loaves was followed by the cutter's forefinger. For several seconds we just stared at it, not fully realizing what had happened. The boy stopped spinning the handle and gazed wide-eyed at his right hand now missing a finger and gushing blood, like a character from *Titus Andronicus*, then without making a sound he went very pale in the face and fell to the ground in a dead faint. The master leaped forward and wrapped a dishcloth around the boy's hand and lifting him in his arms rushed him off to the sickbay, leaving the lifeless finger on the table. One boy rushed from the room and was sick in the yard, but the others who were less squeamish examined it dispassionately like hardened pathologists. I was not particularly upset by the incident, but nor was I over-eager to inspect the severed finger. Tea that day was very late, for all the bread had to be thrown away and the table was scrubbed and sterilized before fresh bread was cut. Some weeks later the boy emerged from the sickbay minus his finger but otherwise none the worse. Perhaps in later life his minor disability turned out to be a blessing in disguise—he would for instance have avoided conscription into the armed forces, for a soldier without a trigger finger would be of no earthly use to the army.

There were often accidents of this kind, though not all were as severe. Climbing trees was a popular pastime, and broken bones sustained from falls were commonplace, boys between the ages of twelve and fourteen being fantastically accident-prone. The most horrifying mishap that I can remember was a boy falling into a bath of scalding tomato soup. It was being carried by two of the kitchen boys along the passage *en route* for the dining hall to be served up for lunch, when suddenly the unfortunate little boy came haring around a corner not looking where he was going, intent no doubt upon being first in the lunch queue. SPLASH he went, head-first into the steaming soup. I cannot remember how badly he was scalded, but his screams of pain were loud enough to wake the dead. There was another boy who fell over and stabbed a school pen straight through the fleshy part of his thigh. We all used to carry our pens and pencils in the tops of our socks, strong elastic garters kept them from falling out – and also cut off the blood circulation to the legs when new!

Within a year of his arrival at the Home Pedro had mastered the English language and though his accent was somewhat halting he was well able to make himself understood. He had been born in the romantic-sounding village of Santa Maria de Corcó in the arid wasteland between Gerona and Vich, some fifty miles from Barcelona. I listened agog as he related to me tales of his war-torn homeland. His father had been killed in action, his brother and he had been saved by the Red Cross and got out of the country, Pedro had come to England, and he thought that his brother was with relations in France but was not sure. I had a little trouble in attaching any credence to his Hemingway-style tales of the civil war, but realize now that every word that he told me was the truth. If I was a problem child he had every licence to be completely out of his skull. But he seemed to accept the tragedy of his life far more easily than I was able to accept mine. I think that this was mainly because he was aware of the tragic circumstances that had led him to the Home and I was not.

Upon his arrival from Spain Pedro had been a Roman Catholic, but Barnardo's, not being over-keen on Catholicism, had converted him to Church of England – well, perhaps converted is too strong a word. He was in any event made to attend the same religious instruction classes as us, and attended the C. of E. church every Sunday. I think he absorbed it and rejected it in the same way that I had. But he had a wonderful singing voice and once sang a solo at the Easter Sunday service. Pedro was also one of the few boys ever to get any mail. I never did find out who the letters were from, but remember being very impressed with having a friend who actually got letters from the outside world.

Pedro had more attributes than anyone I had ever met in my life. He seemed to be able to do everything well, he was good at sport, had learned the language and was also one of the best farters I have ever heard. Farting was a great pastime and Pedro could let rip more or less to order – especially after beans. In the dormitory after lights out, the boys amid raucuous laughter would pick up sides and have roisterous farting matches, the first one to shit himself being the loser. Points were also given for quality, loud rumbustious farts received five points, rapid machine-gun-fire ones three points, everyday undistinguished ones two points, and barely audible ones one point. Points were deducted if a player was unable to score within a minute of it becoming his turn to fart, carpet-slipper or vicarage tea-party efforts were disqualified, so were the ones of those who (unable to control their bowels) blew off out of turn. Pedro was almost always the winner of these tournaments for he could fart all the other competitors off the face of the earth.

It was of course totally against the rules to utter a sound after lights out, but during the farting matches the noise was like Bedlam let loose. The matron, whose room was within earshot of our dormitory, would sometimes creep in unnoticed and put a handful of boys on report. The following morning they would have to parade before the Governor, who never seemed to tire of whipping their hands with his springy bamboo cane.

One day we all got mumps, that is to say several of the boys caught it and spread the epidemic to the rest. It being a disease that you can only catch once in your life, the Governor thought it best that we should all have it at the same time. So the gym was converted into a huge dormitory and all those who had not yet caught it were put in there with those who already had it, and there they were made to stay till they got it. Mumps is not a very serious sickness for children and the swelling of the jowls soon goes down. It is the three weeks that one has to spend in isolation that drags. We had almost nothing to do to pass the time except read and have pillow fights and sometimes real fights. For being cooped together for such a long time was a trying business. It brought out the best and worst in us. I was an incredibly bad patient, I never stopped moaning from morning till night and thoroughly getting on everyone else's nerves. At night when all was quiet I would silently get dressed and creep out of the gym and into the woods. There I would lie on the leafy ground and study the stars; owls hooted in the branches of the trees and nocturnal creatures crept stealthily about in their endless search for food – no doubt they were all very surprised to find themselves with mumps the following morning.

How I loved the woods at night. Never did I have any fear of them, unlike many of the boys who firmly believed the woods to be inhabited by bogey men after dark. I loved to look at the moon on windy nights when clouds raced across it. 'Hey diddle diddle, the cat and the fiddle. The cow jumped over the moon, the little dog run to see such fun, and the dish ran away with the spoon' – I would mutter the doggerel as I gazed up into the night sky.

Then suddenly a twig would snap, quite close to where I was lying. Sometimes a crafty fox would cross my path, his nose glued to his quarry's spoor, then suddenly he would catch a whiff of me and stop dead in his tracks, glance about suspiciously and then jog off once more in pursuit of his prey. A nightingale would start to sing, chirping grasshoppers and hoarse-throated frogs would also join the nocturnal serenade. Often I would drift off into contented sleep and not awake until dawn. Then I would scurry back to the Home before I was missed by the matron.

The freedom of the countryside only served to make the confinement of the institution the more pronounced. How I hated it all, the smell of boys, the cruel staff and above all, I think, the complete lack of privacy. Why on earth did they never ask me what I thought or felt? Why did they not bother to find out what kind of child I was? I could have enlightened them, I am certain of that, and perhaps have given them some sort of insight into how best to handle me. I was utterly and completely starved of love, I needed it more than the stodgy food that I sat down to at every meal. Were they blind? Or did they think that harsh treatment made men of boys? I know that they set great store by toughness and I was as tough as the toughest, indeed on more than one occasion I was downright violent. For this I was thrashed when I should have been kissed. In time I got the message as they knocked all need for affection into my subconscious mind and only the hard veneer of the budding delinquent remained visible. My features hardened into a permanent scowl – a protective shell against all aggressors, one glance into my hardened eyes was enough to make the hardiest quake at the knees. And yet deep inside me was a sensitive human being wanting to love all around me and be loved by them in return. What a different person I might have been if just one of those blind people had noticed it. By the time I was fourteen I was consumed with hate, there was not the slightest room in my soul for anything else.

When I got over mumps I got yellow jaundice. They said that it was from eating too much fat and they could have been right for the stew that we had for lunch at least twice a week was always thick with it. There was always more fat than meat, indeed I have seen more meat on a butcher's apron than I did in those stews. It was a more serious illness than mumps and I was in the sickbay for several weeks, living on dry toast and orange juice most of time.

One Christmas the American Army treated us all to a visit to the pantomime at a theatre in Kingston, it was the *Wizard of Oz*. How excited we all were when two huge Army trucks called to take us. The drivers let the tailboards down and we clambered in, the smaller boys being hoisted aboard by a burly cigar-chewing sergeant, each boy was given a bag of candy and a bottle of Coca-Cola, then off we set, singing 'Bless 'em all, bless 'em all. The long and the short and the tall.' Followed by 'Kiss me Goodnight Sergeant-Major,' and ending up with 'Roll out the Barrel,' by which time we had arrived at the theatre. It was my very first visit to a theatre and how excited I was when the curtain went up on the glittering production. Beautiful girls wearing brilliantly coloured dresses danced about happily with dazzling smiles firmly fixed upon their faces. The grand old wizard entered with flowing beard and robes, the children cheered him till they were hoarse as he got up to one hilarious stunt after another. The plot was somewhat confusing, for every now and then a couple of clowns would come on and pour white-wash over each other or paper a wall in an alarming manner, but in later life when I saw other pantomimes I realized that they did this kind of thing in all of them, as an interlude between one scene and the next. The whole cast sang: 'We're off to see the wizard, the wonderful wizard of Oz, because, because, because, because of the wonderful things he does...' and we joined them, yelling at the tops of our voices. Then a beautiful young girl charmingly sang 'Somewhere over the rainbow skies are blue,' the song which was of course made famous by Judy Garland in the film version of the show. At the end balloons were showered down upon us from a huge net attached to the ceiling and the girls on the stage scattered sweets among us like manna from heaven.

It was a beautiful day, everyone having such a good time and the American soldiers being so kind to us, just like we were ordinary children. But when it was all over and we had to go back to the Home, the treat seemed only to make my bitterness the more acute.

# *Goldings*

WHEN I HAD TURNED FOURTEEN it was decided that since I was so far behind at school, it would not be wise to find me 'a situation.' Instead I was sent to Barnardo's Technical School in Hertfordshire, called Goldings. The administration people fondly hoped that I would learn a trade. On the last day of my final term at the outside school the headmaster summoned me to his office and gave me a pep talk about the evils of loose women, gambling and drink. Having lived an extremely sheltered existence I had not the slightest idea what he was on about so I dismissed all he had to say as utter rot.

On 8th July 1944 I set off for Goldings together with several other boys in a huge lorry with the letters DBH on the side of it; it had come especially from head office to take us on the journey. To my intense delight Pedro was in our number. I am certain that this was not because of any deference the staff might have had for our friendship but because we were near enough the same age.

I was very pleased to be getting away from the dreadful Kingston Home, but might have known that I was leaping straight out of the frying-pan into the fire. For Goldings turned out to be the most fearsome establishment I have ever been in!

Though the Governor was a mild clergyman named MacDonald, the institution was run with a rod of iron. Drill, marching, physical training and cold showers were the order of the day. The PT instructor was the most important man in the place for they adhered insanely to the idiotic adage about healthy bodies having healthy minds. You had to be tough or you went under. Indeed one boy died whilst I was there; it was said to have been from natural causes, but then some causes are more natural than others.

Though I have complained bitterly about the incessant punishment inflicted upon me, the continual moralizing and their apparent inability to understand the first thing about why I was the way I was, etc, I think Barnardo's worst crime was their blatant under-estimation of the intelligence of just about every boy and girl in their care, as a result of which they set their sights low. The only trades that could be learnt at Goldings were carpentry, cobbling, gardening, tinsmithing and printing, the latter being intellectually the most advanced. A boy with a creative streak in his make-up was a dead pigeon from the start. Artistic expression and individuality were squashed as soon as they reared their ugly heads. Certainly the country needed people with these kind of trades, and it may well be that the majority of the boys at Goldings were better suited to a trade than a profession. But certainly it was not true of all and absolutely it was not true of me. Not that I really had the slightest idea what I wanted to do with my life, for indeed I had not. But surely if they had delved into my mind a little they might have got some inkling as to what my capabilities might be. They didn't, so I just went on in the same old way, hating all around me and ultimately hating myself the worst of all.

I spent my first few months there being what they called a 'spare boy', that is to say a boy that they could find nothing to do with. After a time they did try me in the Carpenter's

Shop, in the hope that I would learn a trade. It was useless. I simply could not handle such tools as planes, chisels and tenon-saws. I ruined every exercise that I was given, and was eventually taken out of the course, before I could destroy every last plank of wood they had in the place.

They tried me then in the Bootmakers' Shop. This too ended in desperation and disaster. They told me that I was not trying (I certainly was). It did not occur to them that perhaps I was not cut out to be a craftsman or a tradesman. Their attitude seems to have been: if you cannot learn to be a Carpenter or a Bootmaker you can learn nothing. So they put me in the kitchen, washing dishes and peeling potatoes.

These utilitarian trades were of course extremely beneficial to the other Homes throughout the length and breadth of the country. For the boots made by the cobblers, the chairs and tables made in the carpenter's shop, and the tea cans made by the tinsmiths were all sent to the various Homes in the DBH lorry that called every few weeks loaded with more slave labour and taking away finished work. The compositors printed Barnardo's propaganda as well as all their stationery. Goldings was if nothing else a going concern, employing child labour. The boys were fed, clothed and housed. If they worked hard they got a few coppers pocket money each week, and if they did not they were beaten for idleness, usually by the PT instructor who had biceps many inches in diameter, a shaven head and a sadistic nature. I am certain that he was employed by head office for his expertise with a cane.

The cockroaches in the kitchen outnumbered the boys ten to one. During the day they hid behind the steam coppers out of sight, but at night they ventured forth for a little exercise. If anyone walked across the kitchen floor at night when the lights were out, they would leave a trail of mangled corpses behind them, for the cockroaches covered the floor from wall to wall like a thick pile carpet in a Mayfair penthouse. An attempt or two was made to put them down, but to no avail; they were hardy creatures and defied every insecticide on the market, indeed I think they thrived on them.

At least working in the kitchen I got out of the incessant marching about and being bullied by prefects. I spent so much time in there that I began to smell like a kitchen and look like a dishcloth. The cook was a hard task-master, and inspected my washing-up as closely as a sergeant-major might inspect a squad of recruits. He warned me that every saucepan that I washed was to be wiped *dry*. He would then choose one at random and tell me to hold it upside-down. For every drop of water that dripped out he would strike me on the head with a wooden spoon. This tended to leave me somewhat dazed at times, depending of course upon how many drops of water fell out of the saucepans.

Whilst I mouldered away in the kitchen Pedro was learning carpentry and was within a comparatively short time as near to being a master craftsman as didn't matter. He had also become a member of the football and cricket team, he was greatly liked and highly respected by both staff and boys. Indeed a blue-eyed boy all the way around. Somehow we managed to remain on friendly terms, though the spirit of our friendship, so strong during the early days at Kingston, was severely impaired. I would have liked to have been able to emulate him but my heart just wasn't in it. Often under some duress he would defend me, when the other boys denounced me as useless. But he was fighting a losing battle for there was a great deal of truth in what they said.

I sought and found solace in other directions. Friendship of a kind came to me in the shape of a hulking great lout whom I will call Ginger. Like me Ginger was a misfit, like me he had been dumped in the kitchen out of harm's way. In the normal course of events he would not have been the kind of boy I would have chosen to be friends with, but our plight seemed to be identical and as we stood side by side, our arms up to the elbows in washing-up water for most of our waking hours, there was little chance of avoiding him. Ultimately we were bound to form some sort of alliance.

Ginger was the coarsest boy I had ever met, he was always playing with himself and masturbated nightly after lights out. He made no secret of this, indeed he often boasted about it, saying that when he was on form he could do it three times in a night. No wonder he always looked so haggard. 'Ninety-nine change hands,' he would laugh when he came into the kitchen after a hard night's jerking-off. He would then mime the action with his hand on the outside of his trousers, so as to leave no one in doubt as to what he was referring to. Actually, although we had little contact with girls at Goldings there was very little, if any, homosexuality. But masturbation was rife. Almost all the boys did it, but by and large they were more discreet about it than old Ginger. Now and then he would organize masturbating competitions in the urinal, the winner being the boy who could ejaculate quickest and farthest. Ginger was invariably the winner, indeed I am certain that he could have wanked for Britain in the Olympics and won a gold medal with ease. He was a dirty bastard but you couldn't help liking him. Though no doubt these sporting affairs had to do with our latent sexual frustrations, the boys looked upon it only as a mild joke. However, the staff needless to say did not, and to be caught at it meant a good hiding.

With Ginger as my new friend I now needed no enemies. My association with him was later defined in my dossier as: 'Getting into bad company.' There was nothing new in that: I had been in bad company from the day I had been delivered to the Homes.

・　　・　　・　　・　　・

One Saturday afternoon I was lying about in the recreation hut, when suddenly a prefect appeared and asked me what I was doing. I told him nothing, though in fact I was hanging about in the hope that someone would come in with a cigarette and give me a puff. 'Well, the second eleven football team are one short,' he said.

'So what,' said I.

'So you can play,' said he.

'You must be joking.'

'No I'm not.'

'But I don't know the rules even.'

'That doesn't matter, it's only the second eleven.'

'I don't know how to play.'

'Look,' he said losing patience. 'If you don't play I'll smash your face in.'

'Have it your way,' I shrugged. 'But don't blame me if we lose.'

'There isn't anyone else we can get at such short notice,' he said. 'The rest of the boys have gone off to the pictures.' With a faint heart I followed him to the sports room where he kitted me out with boots, shorts and jersey and then escorted me to the football pitch where the other ten boys waited to play against a local village team. Many derogatory remarks were passed by the other members of the Home team as they saw me approaching. The referee blew his whistle and I reluctantly joined the rest of the boys on the field. The stupid game began. The two teams rushed furiously up and down the field kicking the ball to one another and shouting 'Over here, over here!' Now and then the ball would come near me, and though the uppermost thought in my mind was to run away from it I did kick it once or twice, in no particular direction, for all I wanted to do was get it away from me before I was barged by one of the husky boys from the opposing team. Towards the end of the first half the visitors scored a goal, making them one and us nil. The ball was placed in the centre once more and kicked off, suddenly out of the blue I saw it bouncing in my direction with about six members of the village team charging after it. Taking a few steps forward I gave it a mighty kick and the next thing I knew there was a mighty roar as spectators and both teams shouted 'GOAL!' Sheepishly I looked around and saw that I had deftly kicked the ball into *our own* goal mouth. The goalie stood scratching his head with an astonished expression on his face, and there were many threats of 'Wait till we get you after,' from my fellow-sportsmen in the Home team. At the end of the first half the visitors were two goals up, one of their own and one of mine. During the break I kept well out of harm's way at the other end of the field.

At the commencement of the second half, the captain of our side ordered me in no uncertain terms to keep well out of the way and not to touch the ball, unless there was absolutely no other alternative. I willingly complied with his wishes and confined myself to parts of the field where the ball was not. Within fifteen minutes the Home side had scored two goals; their blood was up and they played like tigers – several fouls were incurred. But the referee (a member of the staff) turned a blind eye to them. The visitors retaliated but were unable to score a third goal. I have to own that the Barnardo Boys put on a fine show, especially as they were playing with one man short, for I was contributing nothing whatever to their success.

Several minutes before the final whistle I stood minding my own business in the penalty area of our goal when suddenly I turned to see the ball cannonading in my direction, with all the members of both sides charging after it. Pedro had often told me of the bullfights of his home land, and at that moment I knew exactly how a *torero* must feel when an enraged bull bears down on him. They were all yelling at the tops of their voices and I would have fled if I had not been riveted to the spot through fear. A member of the opposing side gave the ball a pulverizing kick straight at my face, I put up my hands to protect myself and the ball bounced off them, the force of the kick knocking me to the ground. 'Hand ball!' they yelled in unison. The referee blew his brains out on the whistle and awarded a penalty kick to the villagers. The boys jeered at me and threatened my life as the captain of the other side placed the ball on the penalty spot and thundered the ball into the net. Our goalie had not the slightest chance of saving it for the shot was as true and as straight as an arrow.

The whistle blew, indicating the end of the game and perhaps the end of my life. My head bowed in shame, I ambled along behind my fellows to the showers; no one spoke to me as we entered the wash-house, but the atmosphere was electric and I knew that I was doomed. As we took off our football togs two of them came over to me and became insulting. I tried to explain to them that I had been shanghaied into the game, but although they were well aware of that it seemed to make no difference. Without warning one of them took a swing at me, which caught me on the side of the head and sent me sprawling on the floor. Painfully I staggered to my feet hoping that that was going to be an end to it, but no such luck, the great oaf struck me again and once more I hit the deck. Another of the boys, completely unable to contain himself, pounced on top of me and began to pummel my body. Crouching, I covered my face with my hands as best I could but still suffered considerable damage: 'Okay that's enough,' said the referee who must have been present throughout the whole of the proceedings, but had not bothered to intervene. The boy stopped hitting me and with a black eye, split lip and multiple bruises I staggered to my feet and wandered away quietly by myself without uttering another word. At tea that evening the assembled boys glanced at me askance but no one said a word.

That evening Pedro tried to comfort me, but I was inconsolable so after a time he gave it up as a bad job and left me alone. As I lay on my bed staring at the ceiling, my eyes blinded with tears, I resolved to escape from this inhuman hell-hole. But how and where would I go? I had no money and knew absolutely no one outside the Home, but I did not care, I would abscond and leave the rest to destiny.

When the lights were put out and everyone else in the dormitory was fast asleep I silently got dressed and stole out of the room and down the stairs, my heart pounding fit to burst out of my chest. But all was as still as the grave as I crept unobserved out of the back door of the massive building. Like a cat I stalked in the shadows for fear of being observed by some member of the staff from an upstairs window. But every window in the house was black when I glanced back to have what I hoped would be my last-ever glimpse of the Home. Skirting around the side of the village church I stole into the graveyard and hid for a time behind a tombstone, scanning the main road to freedom beyond. Seeing that all was clear I broke cover and ran hell-for-leather across the road, bounded over a ditch on the other side, scrambled through a hedge into an open field, and dropped to the ground like a commando. For a full minute I lay there, my ears pricked for the slightest sound of someone following me, but there came only the thundering of my heart and the panting of my breath. I got to my feet once more and headed across country, covering mile after mile of cultivated land, waste ground, a mass of bracken several feet deep, and densely wooded areas inhabited by pine trees belonging to the government.

Some hours later I felt that I was now far enough away from the Home to rest. Completely exhausted and frozen to the marrow I slumped to the ground under the shelter of a huge tree. Curling up in a ball for warmth, I fell into fitful sleep, from which I awoke several hours later racked with cramp and famished. I was beginning to wish that I had not embarked on the foolhardy escapade, but there was no turning back now. Determined not to be beaten by the elements I pressed on; it was now light and the sun intermittently broke through the clouds, warming the countryside and my weakening frame. But I had not the slightest idea of the time. Certainly I would have been missed by now, and no doubt search parties would soon be on my trail – with bloodhounds perhaps. I also knew that the police would have been informed so they too would be on the lookout for me. But I would give them a run for their money even if I died in the effort. Indeed I would have quite liked to have been dead at that precise moment. What a bedraggled figure I must have looked as I stumbled blindly on not caring where I ended up, intent only on putting as much distance as possible between me and my oppressors.

Eventually I came upon a farmhouse; cautiously I approached it, keeping to the cover of the neatly trimmed privet hedge. A black shaggy dog chained up in the yard sniffed the air and upon getting my scent began to growl. The farmer's wife appeared in the doorway of the house, looked around and, seeing nothing, told the dog to hush. Stealthily I made my way around to the back of the house and peering through the hedge saw a churn of milk standing by the back door. Moving farther along I came upon a rickety gate which I slowly pushed open, taking care not to let it creak. With my heart in my mouth I slipped inside and crouched behind the mammoth wheel of a farm tractor. Peeking around it to make sure the coast was clear I suddenly threw caution to the winds and raced across the yard to where the milk churn was standing, and with the last of my remaining strength wrenched the lid off it. It came away easily though I almost toppled the churn over in my haste to get at the creamy milk inside. Laying the lid aside I began to scoop up the life-giving liquid in my cupped hands and pour it down my throat – so frenzied was my splashing about that I got more of the milk down the front of my shirt than I did down my gullet. Suddenly as I bent over the churn a huge horny hand landed on my shoulder and a gruff voice with a country accent bellowed: 'Nar then young fella-me-lad, what you up to?' I swung around and found myself looking into the weather-beaten face of a farm worker. At the sound of his voice the dog set to barking, thereby raising the alarm. The farmer came running out of the house followed closely by his ample wife.

'What be goin' on 'ere then?' asked the farmer.

'Caught this young shaver drinkin' o' the milk,' replied the labourer, still keeping a tight hold of my arm. I tried to pull away from him but I had no strength left, I had no other alternative but to capitulate. So I ceased my struggling and told them that I had run away from the Home and had been out all night: 'I only took the milk because I was thirsty,' I pleaded as I observed the stern expressions on the faces of the two men.

'Poor little mite,' exclaimed the farmer's wife, her maternal instincts coming to the fore. 'Bring him into the house this minute.'

'If'n I letcha go willya run away?' asked the rustic.

'No sir,' I promised.

'All right then you go on in the 'ouse wiv the missus.' He let me go and I followed the fat lady into the house, her husband bringing up the rear, no doubt to make sure I did not break my word about not making a run for it.

The interior of the house was as you might expect – spotlessly clean whitewashed walls, white wood furniture in the kitchen worn from years of scrubbing. The fragrant aroma of newly baked bread made my savage hunger the more acute.

'Sit down son?' smiled the farmer's wife. 'You must be starving.'

'I am, madam,' I replied dolefully and plonked myself down on a chair.

'Where did you run away from, son?' asked the farmer in a kindly tone.

'Goldings,' I said fearfully.

'Bless me that's more'n ten mile away,' said the wife throwing bacon into the sizzling pan. 'How many eggs could you eat dear?' I could have eaten a dozen but told her that one would do. 'Bless me, one's not enough for a growing lad,' she roared, her fat bosom wobbling with amusement. 'You will have three my lad and not a scrap do I want to see left.' Here in the heart of England life went on undisturbed by the war, country folk were virtually untouched by the scarcities of basic essentials. In the towns and blitzed areas eggs and butter were hard to come by and fetched grotesque sums on the black market. But in the sleepy villages tranquillity and abundance went hand in hand.

Soon my breakfast was cooked and laid before me; it was indeed the finest sight I have seen, before or since. After looking at it for several seconds in disbelief I got tucked into it without delay. Unnoticed by me the farmer discreetly left the room and phoned the local police station to tell them that I was at the farm, so that the search could be called off and they could come for me. Within a few minutes I had consumed every last morsel on my plate and had wiped it spotlessly clean with great slabs of newly baked bread. How pleased the farmer's wife was to see me eat. 'Poor little lad,' she said, placing an outsized cup of steaming chocolate in front of me 'I bet they half starve them up at that place.'

'Now then me dear, it ain't our business,' said the farmer

who had returned to the kitchen and had seated himself opposite me at the table.

'Well I think it's too bad, that's all,' she sighed.

'Now, now,' said the man.

I did not know that the police had been sent for and suspected nothing as they questioned me about life in the Homes, and inquired about where I had come from originally. I was totally unable to enlighten them about my antecedents for I did not know the answer, but I was more than willing to relate gruesome tales about life in Barnardo's. When asked how I had sustained my black eye I told them truthfully what had happened and both were visibly shocked. All too soon the police car arrived to take me away, I glanced about frantically looking for some means of escape as the two coppers entered the kitchen – seeing none I slumped back in my chair and reconciled myself to my fate.

'Well, you've been leading us a merry dance,' said one of the policemen, smiling benignly. 'We've been scouring the countryside for you since early morning.' I glanced up at them meekly but made no reply.

'Will you have a cup of tea?' asked the lady, glancing at the policemen.

'That would be nice missus,' replied one of them.

'Good I'll put the kettle on.' I was reprieved for a time at least, but it was short-lived; all too soon it was time to go. The policemen were very friendly as they led me to the car and the farmer's wife was near to tears. I tried desperately to put a brave face on it as I thanked the couple for their kindness to me and did not break down entirely until the car was spinning along the country lanes *en route* for the Home. 'Now now, lad, it can't be as bad as all that,' said the copper sitting next to me in a friendly tone. But his face was sad, I feel sure he knew what was in store for me when they got me back. At a village sweetshop the driver stopped the car and bought me a bar of chocolate. 'Eat it before we get there, there's a good boy,' he said with a smile. Amid floods of tears I ate the chocolate but did not enjoy it; on top of the huge breakfast it made me feel rather sick.

As the car turned into the main drive I stopped snivelling, and sat in the back seat in sullen silence. We drew up outside the front door and several of the boys clustered around to peer at me through the window of the car; the policemen shooed them away and led me inside. The Governor thanked them for their trouble and they departed, the older of the two giving me a reassuring pat on the head as he passed by. When they had gone, the Governor turned his attentions to me. 'You're filthy,' he said turning away in disgust. 'Wait there,' he remarked glancing at me over his shoulder, then stalked into his office. I heard him pick up the 'phone but not what he said. A few minutes later two prefects arrived on the scene and escorted me to the bath house, where I was given what they called a 'regimental scrubbing'. I was ordered by the two boys to strip naked, they then pushed me under a cold shower and scrubbed me with stiff yard brooms, 'like I was an elephant'. The needle-sharp spines of the broom-heads tore my flesh like thorns, but I uttered not a sound. This I think unnerved them somewhat, for without screams of pain they did not enjoy their work. Soon they threw the brooms aside and told me to get dressed, when I had done so they escorted me back to the Governor's office.

'Do you have anything to say?' asked the usually mild clergyman in an angry tone as I stood before his desk. I made no reply. 'Answer me when I speak to you boy,' he demanded, his knuckles going white as he gripped the arms of his chair.

'I have nothing to say,' I mumbled.

'Speak up,' he roared. I remained silent.

'I will not have this dumb insolence,' he said leaping to his feet. I thought for a moment that he was going to strike me and took a pace backwards. 'You will be flogged at evening assembly,' he said in a tone belying the calling of the collar around his neck. 'Now go and stand in the passage outside.' I turned and left the room. All day long I stood in the passage awaiting the inevitable. Now and then a boy would pass by with his eyes averted, for they had no taste for what they were going to be compelled to witness that evening. During the afternoon Pedro sneaked along the passage and handed me a thick sandwich which he had concealed beneath his coat. They had not allowed me in to lunch.

'Keep your cheen up,' he said in his thick Spanish accent, 'they cannot keel you.' I smiled weakly, I had less confidence than he as to what they would stop short of.

The afternoon dragged on and though I was sick with fear I resolved that I would show none when the moment of my ordeal arrived. The boys went in to tea and afterwards two prefects came for me. I was led into the hushed dining-hall and stood facing the three hundred boys. The Governor rose to his feet and mounted the rostrum; for a long moment he glared at me coldly then turned to the assembled boys.

'This boy is a disgrace to the good name of this establishment,' he began vehemently, 'an absolute disgrace. I will not tolerate this kind of behaviour. . . .' He continued for several minutes in censorious tone then roaring like Captain Bligh he sentenced me to: 'Six strokes of the cane, to be well laid on.' The PT instructor stepped forward and flayed the air with his trusty cane several times menacingly. Then he ordered me to bend over. Mutely I obeyed, the rod swished the air once more – the odious ritual had begun. I did not flinch as the first of the blows landed squarely on the seat of my short pants, followed swiftly by the second and third. Still I uttered no cry of pain. Incensed by his inability to make me scream for mercy, he administered the fourth stroke with such force that I lost my balance and fell to my knees. For a few seconds

I did not move, a murmur of complaint rippled around the hall as I painfully dragged myself to my feet, first crouching on all fours then clutching at the rostrum for support, gritting my teeth I determinedly remained silent. My backside was now numb and I hardly felt the fifth and sixth lashes. The ignominious flagellation now well and truly administered, I stood erect and faced the assembly. I knew that I had acquitted myself well and that this would be a day that no one, staff or boys, would forget in a hurry.

Though I had been the immolated victim I had, through showing no cowardice or tears, won the day. From now on I knew that I would be respected by the boys, the prefects would no longer pick on me and even the staff would think twice before punishing me again. Such is the stupidity of human nature.

'He has problems and I am anxious about his future,' states the Governor in a letter to head office about me. This excessively witty observation comes as no surprise to me whatever.

For a time after this life went on fairly uneventfully, my behaviour did not improve or get worse – it remained about the same, but they left me alone. Though I was just about able to read and write my orthography and grammar were unorthodox to say the least of it. Indeed I have never been able to master either of them proficiently. One or two afternoons a week I attended classes and a desperate attempt was made to improve my education, but my lethargy and lack of co-operation made all hope of progress futile. In the end the teacher gave up and I just sloshed about in the kitchen day after day week in week out, waiting for the day that they would let me go, for that they would certainly have to do after my sixteenth birthday.

I contributed to the war effort during this period by volunteering to be a guinea-pig for the Ministry of Health. Among the million things that there was a shortage of was toothpaste. Ministry scientists had discovered after many months of research that negroes in Jamaica all had marvellous teeth in spite of the fact that they had never found the need to use toothpaste – excepting in sandwiches perhaps. Upon closer investigation it was discovered that the Jamaicans kept their teeth sparkling by daily gnawing on sticks of sugarcane. It was thought that if the chewing of sugarcane had the same effect on white people as it did on coloured, thousands of tons of it could be imported and distributed to the troops, whose teeth it seems were suffering greatly from decay due to the acute shortage of toothpaste.

A ministry dentist called at the Home one day and inspected the teeth of all the boys and wrote down the names of those with the dirtiest. Mine was among them, indeed I would not be at all surprised if mine were not at the top of the list. For my teeth in those days looked like gorgonzola cheese, caused by neglect and a lack of calcium in our diet. When asked if I would be willing to take part in the experiment I was more than delighted to volunteer; for on the face of it there seemed to be nothing that I could lose, excepting perhaps a few teeth, which no doubt I would have been a lot better off without anyway.

Each morning I was given a great lump of succulent sugarcane to chew on and told that under no circumstances was I to use a tooth-brush. The boys with good teeth were extremely jealous of those with bad. For a few days I conscientiously chewed on the stuff but was not over-keen on the taste of it. One day a boy offered me a cigarette in exchange for my morning stick of sugarcane and without the slightest hesitation I agreed to the trade, firmly convinced that I was getting the best of the deal. Every morning after that I swopped my unexpected perquisite for cigarettes. The experiment was to go on for a month, at which time the ministry dentist would visit the Home to see how much improvement there was in the condition of our teeth. As the date of his arrival drew near, I began to scour my teeth frantically with salt mixed with tooth powder; the results were staggering for my teeth, once brown, became a dazzling white. Indeed they could hardly have been bettered by a film star.

When the day of inspection arrived the dentist was so pleased with the improvement in the condition of my teeth, that he commended me to the governor for my zealous cooperation. The experiment had been a success but as far as I know the ministry's report was not put into effect. (Twenty years later I had my teeth capped. With showbiz money.)

The highest honour that could be bestowed on a boy at Goldings was to be made a prefect: a boy would have to 'excel at sport' or be 'of exemplary character'. For a prefect there were many perks (being allowed to stay up later than the rest of the boys, use of the prefect's room, in which there was a billiard-table and dart-board; they were also permitted to smoke, though I do not think that this was official). It was also the prefects who were usually chosen to go to Wimbledon, to act as ball boys at the famous tennis tournaments. But their greatest privilege was that they could place any boy on report whom they caught breaking one of the hundred-and-one rules. They could also, within reason, inflict the punishment themselves. It was no joke if a prefect had it in for you, particularly if it happened to be the school captain who, like the other great dictators of our day, had omnipotence.

It is extraordinary how changed a boy could become once he had been elevated to the hierarchy. He would immediately drop all his old friends and join the ranks of the establishment. Very often they would abuse their authority and become tyrannical bullies; they were feared and loathed by the other boys, but not one of them would have turned down the promotion had it been offered him. Even Pedro became a prefect; he however did not take advantage of his power, certainly not with me anyway.

On Saturday afternoon we were sometimes allowed to visit the market town of Hertford about three miles away. It was quite a treat for it was the only glimpse we ever got of the outside world. After lunch, dressed in grey flannels and green Barnardo's blazers, we would set off under threat of dire punishment if we were not back by five o'clock tea. There not being a bus route from the Home to the town we usually had to walk; it was against the rules to hitch a lift, but it was a rule often broken. Most of the boys made a bee-line for the Odeon cinema where in those days half-price front stalls could be got for ninepence. We paid our money at the box-office and had our tickets torn in half by a pretty usherette, half the ticket she retained and half was handed back to us, so that the girl inside would know which price seats to put us in. After a few visits to the picture house I discovered that if I got two halves of a torn ticket and meticulously stuck them together with thin sticky paper, the girl on the door could not tell the difference between the forgery and a newly purchased ticket, for she never looked very closely at them and was anyway in the dark. I knew from bitter experience that it would have been unwise to tell any of the other boys about the fiddle, so I kept it to myself and was never caught.

In the summer I would go for long walks in the country, sometimes with Pedro or Ginger but more often alone. For now that Pedro was a prefect we hardly ever spoke to each other any more, an almost insuperable gulf had come between us. Outside the grounds we could recapture some semblance of our former friendship, but inside relations were strained for we were caught between opposite poles. Ginger on the other hand was trouble and though he was often entertaining I avoided him like the plague most of the time. For although

I was obviously a difficult case myself I preferred to make my own bed to lie on.

On one of our rare outings together Pedro and I spied two pretty young country girls sitting on a gate. As we approached they giggled coyly and brazenly called to us. Cautiously we drew near to them. I was fantastically bashful of girls in those days (and still am, though I now manage to cover it up extraordinarily well). As we came abreast of them I was acutely embarrassed when they suddenly barred our way and demanded a kiss as toll to go through the gate. They were out for a lark and had dared each other to kiss the next boy that came along (the boys from the Home often passed that way).

Going as red as a beetroot I tried to climb over the gate without giving a kiss, but one of the girls grabbed hold of me and pulled me off. I glanced around and saw Pedro meekly submitting to the ordeal in the arms of the other girl. The girl who had pulled me off the gate bore down on me and threw her arms around my neck.

'Leave off,' I exclaimed trying to push her away.

'Don't be silly,' she replied smashing her lips against mine, my struggles were in vain for she had me firmly pinioned against the bars of the gate, the full weight of her body pressed on top of me. Gasping for breath I eventually made my escape, vaulted the gate and ran for my life across a field, with the girl in hot pursuit. Glancing over my shoulder I saw Pedro sitting on a grass bank, his arm about the waist of the other girl; both were laughing fit to bust.

None of us had noticed a 'BEWARE OF THE BULL' notice obliterated from sight by an overhanging branch of a tree by the gate. The flashing colours of the girl's summer frock must have caught his attention, for he suddenly appeared from under the shade of an elm tree, snorting and pawing the ground. Pedro jumped on the gate and yelled to us to watch out as the lumbering beast, his head down, suddenly rampaged after us. We had a good start but he was rapidly gaining on us. The girl screamed and tripped over a clod of earth and fell to the ground. Seeing that she was in grave danger Pedro leapt over the gate, rushed across the field waving his blazer and yelling '*Toro! Toro!*' The bull came to a dead stop about twenty-five yards away from where the girl was lying and menacingly turned in Pedro's direction. The Spanish boy showing no fear continued to advance upon the bull, shouting '*Toro bravo! Toro bravo!*' and taunting him with his blazer. The bull then charged at Pedro but was ridiculously outclassed. Pedro laughing his head off zigzagged around the field, thoroughly confusing the beast who in the end gave up and trotted off to a corner of the field by himself. Approaching him cautiously, his blazer spread like a cape in front of him, Pedro goaded and insulted the bull mercilessly, the savage-tempered beast bellowed fiercely but would not be drawn into battle.

'*Toro de paja*,' remarked Pedro in disgust and turning his back on the defeated animal walked triumphantly across the field to where we were quaking with fear behind the safety of the gate.

'*Toro de paja*,' (bull of straw) he said again in a disgusted tone of voice as he mounted the gate and dropped nimbly to the ground the other side. Pedro had been an *aficionado* almost from birth – bull-fighting was in his blood and he was extremely disappointed at the cowardliness of his very first opponent. A disgrace to the national sport of his homeland. I smiled when this incident came to mind many years later when I was watching bull-fights in Madrid and Granada.

The girl's names were Janet and Mary, both were beautiful and in their early teens. Janet was Pedro's girl friend and Mary was mine, each Saturday afternoon that we were allowed out we went to meet them. Sometimes we took them to the pictures, at other times we took them for long walks in the country. I cannot say that I was in love with Mary in the way I had been with Irene or the wild-eyed Hilda May at the Bedford Home, nor even in the same way as with Miss Love, for they will forever be set apart. But I liked her a lot and tolerated her perpetual giggling, though it irritated me considerably at times. Having suffered the ignominy of my first real kiss, I soon got an insatiable desire for it. Mary had beautifully soft pouting lips, which filled me with the most delicious sensations whenever they touched mine. The four of us would lie behind haystacks or in the long grass and neck till our bodies ached and our lips were sore. The idea of doing anything more carnal simply did not occur to us. Our speciality was the long-drawn-out kiss, well over a minute in duration; not realizing that it was permissible to breathe during a kiss I would hold my breath the whole time that my lips were against Mary's. When at last the kiss came to an end with a juicy report, I would flake out on the grass, blue in the face and gasping.

During this period Pedro and I became close friends once more and though it endangered his position as a prefect he now fraternized with me as much within the precincts of the Home as he did when we were out with our girls. And when after several weeks Mary announced that she was in love with me, and demanded that I see her more than once a week, Pedro covered for me when I stole away in the dead of night to meet her. Sometimes he even came with me to meet Janet, thus putting himself in grave peril.

One night I crept off to meet Mary without telling Pedro. Of late Mary and I had been talking a good deal about sex, we both wanted to do it but were too frightened – we had not said so in so many words, but the yearning in our kisses and the reaction of our bodies when pressed close together told us all we needed to know. I vowed that that night I would *do* her and be done with it. We always met at the same place by a rustic bridge just beyond the boundary of the grounds, out of the shadows she appeared and flew into my arms as I approached her, our lips meeting in a rhapsodic kiss. Gently we lay together on the ground, stroking and kissing in frenzied excitement. Suddenly my hand was beneath her dress, fumbling with her knickers. She made no complaint nor attempt to stop me as I slid them down over her tight little buttocks and then farther down to her knees, suddenly, bringing her legs up she assisted in divesting herself of them the rest of the way. 'We shouldn't,' she said as I rolled on top of her. By way of reply I showered her with kisses. We were virgins together, neither of us versed in the art of lovemaking, simply working from natural instincts. We both wanted but feared it. Suddenly, more by luck than from good judgement, I entered her, it hurt her and she cried aloud. She dug her fingernails into my shoulders and in the moonlight I saw that she bit her lower lip in order to stifle her cries of pain. In less than a minute I had experienced the most ecstatic sensation of my life. We had broken each other in. After a time I rolled off her.

Mary glanced in my direction but could not look me in the eye; to comfort her I held her very close to me and muttered hardly audible endearments in her ear.

'I must get home darling,' she said stroking my hair.

'I suppose so,' I replied, reluctantly loosening my grip on her.

'You won't tell anyone will you,' she said pulling her knickers on and smoothing her dress down.

'Of course not,' I exploded, suddenly appalled at the idea of being found out.

After several more passionate kisses, and reciprocal assurances of undying love, we parted company till the following Saturday. I ran back to the Home and managed to sneak in unobserved. At reveille the following morning I found to my horror that there was blood all over the front of my short trousers. I took Pedro aside and told him that I had torn a great hole in my shorts (a punishable offence). Without asking questions he hied himself to the stores and pinched me another pair. The others I hid under my mattress till everyone was at work, then I stole up to the dorm, tore my name tab out of them and threw them in the rubbish-bin. I then crept guiltily back into the kitchen, hardly able to believe that I had actually managed to get away with something.

True to my word I did not tell a soul that I had fucked Mary, but how I looked forward to Saturday afternoons. So as to cause no suspicion I continued to accompany Pedro when we went to meet the girls, but usually managed to get Mary behind a haystack for a 'bit of the other', before the end of the afternoon. In the pictures we groped and kissed each other madly.

One day as we headed home, after seeing the girls, Pedro sheepishly confided that he had poked Janet some days before. Convulsed with laughter I told him that I had done the same to Mary. He laughed as raucously as I, for it was indeed hilarious that we should both be harbouring the same dark secret. Throwing our arms around each other's shoulders we strolled up the drive, like blood brothers (which indeed we were in a sense). We swore to keep each other's confidence, and parted company as close friends as any two boys can be. He went off to the prefects' room and I to the kitchen to wash dishes.

Now that I was getting my oats regularly Mary somewhat unexpectedly became rather demanding and more than a little mercenary. She insisted on the best seats in the cinema and tea afterwards, these she considered just deserts for her undying love for me. Never could it be said of me that I am close with a penny, but her requirements were simply beyond my means. For on one shilling and sixpence a week I could barely pay for us to get into the pictures in the cheapest seats. There was nothing for it but that I must supplement my income in some way, or run the risk of her going off me. Now that she was no longer a virgin the world was her oyster, she would be able to find herself a better proposition than me without the slightest difficulty.

I gave the matter several days' thought and decided that the quickest and easiest way of making extra money was to go scrumping, for there was always a market for apples which could be sold for a penny each – twopence for large ones. If caught it was a caning matter, but all in all the risk seemed worth taking. A few days later as Ginger and I stood shoulder to shoulder washing the infernal dishes, I mentioned my plan to him, for although I could have gone scrumping on my own it was really a two-handed job. A second man was needed to climb the trees and shake the fruit down whilst the other gathered it up into a sack; with two the burden was easier to carry home and the haul could be greater.

Ginger, having even more larceny in his soul than I, leapt at the idea and said that he knew of an orchard not too far distant that had fruit in abundance. So that very evening during the recreation period we set out on our apple-stealing expedition. Between six o'clock and lights out at nine we would not be missed; according to Ginger that would be ample time to make it there and back.

The orchard was something under a mile away and by keeping to footpaths and stalking behind hedges we managed to avoid the main roads, thus minimizing our chances of capture before reaching our destination.

'It's not far now,' smiled Ginger as we jogged along at a steady trot.

'Is there a dog there?' I asked, the idea occurring to me for the first time.

'Not that I've seen,' said Ginger, his face still wreathed in smiles. He was enjoying himself immensely, this kind of caper being right up his street – in later life he would be a national hero or rot in prison an ignominious criminal, it would depend entirely on Kismet.

Soon we reached the orchard and, dropping on our bellies scanned the terrain for signs of anyone about. All was clear, so without delay we scrabbled under a hedge and Ginger shinned up the nearest tree with the agility of an orang-outang. Gripping the trunk of the tree by one hand and shaking the branches with the other made him look even more like our closest relations in the animal world. The apples rained down on me like cannon balls and I had to call to him to take it easy as I scrambled on the ground picking them up and putting them into a potato sack that we had borrowed from the kitchen. 'There's a pear tree over there,' shouted Ginger, swinging to the ground and racing to another tree near by. Pears were certainly better than apples and fetched a better price from the boys. I left the apples and dragging the sack behind me I chased after him, up the tree he went and down came a shower of juicy ripe pears. As fast as I could I filled the sack, then called to him that we had enough. Immediately he swung to the ground, filled his shirt with the remaining fruit, and took hold of one end of the sack whilst I took hold of the other; we made off with our booty as fast as our legs would carry us.

In spite of our heavy load, we covered the distance home in less time than it had taken us to make the outward-bound journey. Fear of being caught had sped us on. We got back into the grounds unobserved and hid our sackful of fruit under a pile of dead leaves near the dell (which was also used as a rubbish tip). We took back only those that Ginger had in his shirt. The bugler was sounding the Last Post as we entered the back door and ran up the stairs to the dormitory, the operation had gone off without a hitch, almost as though it had been planned by the joint chiefs of staff. How elated I was as I lay on my back munching a gigantic pear when the other boys had gone to sleep.

The following morning we were open for business – cash only, no credit, and do not ask for it for a refusal often offends. What a marvellous costermonger Ginger was; taking the sack of fruit round the back of the recreation hut be began to do a roaring trade. Several boys were employed as lookouts, in case any masters or prefects should come in sight, but all was clear and within half an hour he had sold the lot; apples a penny each, pears twopence, huge ones threepence. Later in the kitchen we had a count-up and share-out; we made over seven shillings, which we split down the middle. The following Saturday Mary would be able to have her heart's desire.

Having got away with it the first time Ginger and I got big eyes and tried it a second. Miraculously, again we were not caught; pushing our luck we raided the orchard a third time and were caught red-handed by the owner who was lying in wait for us with a great big dog. We tried to make a run for it but were held at bay by the vicious-looking brute. Terrified that the dog would tear us to bits, we gave ourselves up meekly and were escorted back to the Home by the man with his canine protector in close attendance. Once more I found myself standing in the passage outside the religious martinet's study waiting to be whipped. Ginger was called in first and after a pause there came the sound of the cane dusting his seat, the first two strokes brought no sound but the last four were accompanied by cries of pain. Red-eyed and tearful the cowardly Ginger emerged from the room and I was called inside. After the usual censorious lecture the Governor much to my consternation gave me a choice of punishment. Either I could have six strokes of the cane in the normal way across the seat of my trousers or alternatively I could drop my trousers and receive three slaps with the flat of his hand on my bare bottom. Thinking that the latter would be the less painful I made that my choice (perverted implications did not occur to me at the time). I touched my toes and he administered the three stinging slaps in rapid succession, as I hitched my pants up I saw that his lower lip trembled and beads of sweat moistened his forehead.

The following morning I absconded again, this time with Ginger as companion. As before we had no destination in mind. To get away from the frightful place was our only object. We walked for miles across the ploughed fields and pastures where cattle grazed. By late afternoon we were tired, hungry and soaked to the skin, for it had been raining intermittently all day long. Then as we rounded a bend in a country lane, we saw a farm wagon parked by the wayside and decided to investigate. Our hope was to find some food. As we clambered into the back of the wagon, we noticed a man working in the fields some way off. He was totally absorbed in whatever it was he was doing and did not see us. I do not remember which one of us it was that found the man's jacket, but suddenly there it was in our hands. We wasted no time in rifling the pockets. We found a packet of cigarettes and a wallet containing some papers, a few photographs and a ten-shilling note. Without hesitation we pocketed the money and cigarettes and ran away.

Later that evening we were stopped by a policeman who questioned us about who we were and where we had come from. Now completely exhausted, we told him and were taken to the police station. The farm-hand must have reported the theft. For no sooner had we entered the police station than we were searched by a sergeant, who found the note in one of our pockets. We grudgingly confessed to the crime, were charged, and appeared in court the following morning. After the reading of the evidence, we stood petrified before the Magistrate who inveighed against us mercilessly and then somewhat surprisingly adjourned the case for three months for a 'Report on the Conduct and Progress of the Boys.' Ginger was hastily transferred to another Home. (I have not seen nor heard from him, from that day to this.) I was given my very last chance.

Upon being returned to the Home the Governor summoned me to his study. I was decidedly alarmed when for the first time he spoke kindly to me, telling me that the incident was now closed but that I had really had my last chance. Much to my amazement he then asked me what I would like to do. I immediately said that I would like to work in the gardens; I had had enough of the kitchen. He agreed that I should be transferred to the gardening party forthwith, but warned me again about the consequences of failure, though he did not say what they would be. What could they be? How could I know? In my dossier he states that he thought I was laughing at him up my sleeve. Was I? I cannot recall.

Work in the gardens had far more to do with agriculture than with horticulture. We felled trees, rolled the cricket pitch, dug the ground and humped hundredweight sacks of potatoes. It was back-breaking work, how miserable I was that I was being trained to be a carthorse instead of a floriculturist.

For a time after the court case I was confined to the grounds, the staff and prefects kept a close eye on me so I had absolutely no chance of slipping away unnoticed, to meet Mary. She was not at all pleased when Pedro told her what I had done. She sent me a few love letters via Pedro saying that she would wait for me, but they soon stopped coming and the relationship just petered out

8th May 1945 was VE day and 15th August the same year was VJ day. The war was over. There was much jubilation, but it didn't seem to affect us overmuch; for many months now we had hardly been aware that it was still going on. In celebration we went to a Summer camp that year at Saint Mary's Bay on the Kent coast. It was the first time I had seen the sea for many years and my longing to serve 'seven years before the mast' and visit exotic oriental ports became unbearably acute. It was to be an ambition never fulfilled. (Perhaps it is still not too late.)

It was during this holiday that I had my second sexual experience, with a fat girl guide inside a smelly disused pillbox up against the wall. It was not much of a conquest but nevertheless something to boast about to the other boys, whose reaction I remember was one of disgust mixed with a slight tinge of envy. Actually in those days I aspired to be a satyr and thought only of girls from dawn to dusk. Pubescence was well and truly upon me

During the last months that I was incarcerated in Goldings, I was left more or less to my own devices. They no longer punished me and indeed ignored my general behaviour, which was by no means exemplary. I had I suppose won the battle which had been raging for just under ten years, but it was an ignoble victory. They had merely given up on me, they had tried force without success. And I think in their opinion they had tried kindness and failed. Giving a demented boy a 'last chance' under threat of 'dire consequences of failure' hardly constitutes loving kindness. And that I think is the crux of the matter; as stated earlier I do not entirely blame Barnardo's for the mental anguish of my childhood and early youth, for no doubt the seeds were sown at birth. But their system only served to nurture my lamentable mental condition which manifested itself in violence, hate and appalling loneliness, stemming from deep-rooted insecurity. (The residue of which remains with me to this day. It will stay till I die, I expect.) The less apparent side-effects of my upbringing are almost too numerous to name: EGOMANIA! CRIMINALITY! INTOLERANCE! TIMIDITY! MEGALOMANIA! MISANTHROPY! are but a few. Many of these grey-matter derangements I have succeeded in bringing under control, and some I have exorcized completely. But there is still an uncontrollable expression of distrust in my eyes when I am introduced to someone for the first time, particularly women. As a matter of fact, though I am entirely heterosexual, I have never had a really successful relationship with a member of the opposite sex. God knows I have had enough goes at it. The trouble is that when I embark on a brand-new affair, the paramount thought in my head is of the pain I am going to suffer when it is over. I am not deluded into thinking that it is the fault of women that I am the way I am, for though I deplore the lack of love in the world, it now becomes a moot point as to whether I am capable of it myself. My friendships with men, however, seem to be made of sterner stuff, because emotionally I have less to lose if they go wrong, I suppose.

# *My Situation*

QUITE UNPREPARED FOR IT I was released from Barnardo's care on 17th October 1946. The DBH lorry arrived to take me to head office where I would be kitted out with bare essentials. An ill-fitting suit, shoes, two shirts, two sets of underclothes, socks, working boots and overalls, etc. I was then photographed. A Barnardo's Welfare Officer escorted me on the train to Waltham Cross on the borders of Greater London and Hertfordshire – indeed it was not that many miles away from Goldings. He took me to the house of a tyranical woman, whom I can only describe as a professional landlady. The house was by no means clean and smelt revoltingly of boiled cabbage. I was to share a small bedroom with two other ex-Barnardo Boys and pay thirty shillings a week board and lodging. There were many rules to be strictly observed: no smoking in the house, clean the bath out, make your own bed, be home by ten at night or be locked out till morning. The dear lady never tired of telling us how unwanted we were and how lucky we were to be taken under her roof. She fed us filthy food and I am certain she made a fair profit out of the money we paid her each week. Conditions were foul, far worse than in any of the Homes.

I was found a situation in a Tomato Nursery near by and

set to earning my own living, the pay being under three pounds a week. Barnardo's remained my legal guardians till I came of age, but to all intents and purposes I was now on my own. The dossier was complete: the final entry documented their continuing anxiety about their difficulty in getting any co-operation from me, and the fact that I was unsettled. But all that was over now, no more moralizing, no more thrashings, no more fear of retribution. I could now actively abandon religion. I had discarded it emotionally for years, but church parade on Sunday had been compulsory.

A new era had begun, a new adventure. I would now be able to extend myself, my time of being cooped up was over, I would spread my wings and fly. But it was not to be so, at least not for a while. I found that I was now in another prison, that of the dreadful job and the uncomforting digs. Each morning I got up at the crack of dawn (before first light in the winter) and after munching a miserable lump of bread and margarine I trundled off to the nursery. Work began at seven sharp – to clock in at three minutes past meant fifteen minutes docked from your pay at the end of the week. It was menial work; when I didn't spend the day up to my arse in horse manure, I spent it almost choking to death on fumigatory chemicals, which burned my eyes and ate into the very fibre of my clothing. These were the only jobs that Barnardo Boys were trusted with. (I was not the only Old Goldolian working there.)

But at week-ends I would escape from it all. Dressed far from elegantly in my discharge suit, I promenaded up and down Waltham Cross High Street in search of life and excitement. How very disappointing life can be at times: it was the dullest place on earth. I was very envious of the sartorial splendour of the local boys' clothes. Draped suits were just coming into fashion worn with white cutaway collars, loudly coloured ties and crêpe-soled shoes an inch thick – known as 'creepers'. They had all the girls, I did not get so much as a look in. I vowed that one day I would acquire such an *ensemble* and devastate the world. But it was not to be, for on my meagre wages it was all I could do to keep body and soul together. Indeed before long my clothes began to wear out, and due to lack of funds I was entirely unable to buy new ones. I polished the uppers of my best shoes to an immaculate shine, but the soles wore right down to my rotting socks; I bought cheap rubber 'stick-on' soles but alas there was nothing to stick them to, so I tin-tacked them to the uppers as best I could. But they became extremely painful to walk in, for the nails pierced the instep of my feet, no matter how meticulously I hammered the sharp ends down. I refused to be beaten, it occurred to me if I took the soles off and nailed them on through the welts on the outside of the shoe towards the ground, and turned the ends over, they would stay on and I would no longer suffer agony walking in them. But though I managed after considerable difficulty to execute the work, the unique discovery was not worth patenting. The shoes turned into spiked track pumps and attached themselves to all manner of supple surfaces, such as linoleum, carpets and asphalt roads. They also scratched woodwork. But my tenacity was insuperable, the next brilliant idea was to sew the soles on with fuse-wire; to my intense satisfaction this worked admirably. But by this time the poor shoes had taken such a beating that they gave up the ghost entirely after only two more outings. At the time of their demise I was jitter-bugging with a girl at the local youth club, to the strains of a jazzed-up recording of a number entitled *'A' You're Adorable*. It was prelude to a lifetime of embarrassing situations with girls.

I had from the beginning hated the woman with whom I had been sent to live. But I remained taciturn and sullen for fear of falling foul of her – I honestly thought she had the power to have me returned to the Home if I misbehaved. But the inevitable day of rebellion came after I had been with her for some three months. Predictably the row was over the disgusting food that she gave us to eat. I came home one evening after a hard day's work on the dung-heap, and she shoved before me a plate of stew which in colour and consistency was more than a little reminiscent to the stuff that I had been shovelling all day.

'What's this muck?' I demanded, glowering up at the woman.

'It's your supper,' she said angrily, 'eat it up and be thankful.'

'You eat it,' I said, pushing it away from me and getting up from the table.

'I shall report you to the Welfare Officer,' she retorted.

'Let me give you something to report me for,' I shouted picking the plate up off the table and hurling the lot at the wall. 'We don't want your goshy plonk so stick it on the wall,' I laughed as the revolting mess slithered down the flowered wallpaper. It was a stupid but effective insult.

'Get out of here this minute!' she roared, coming after me round the table waving a wooden spoon. Without more ado I ran out of the room and upstairs to bed.

The following evening when I returned from work, the Welfare Officer was sitting in an armchair in the living-room.

'Now then lad,' he said in a not particularly unfriendly tone of voice. 'What's all the trouble about?' I glanced at the woman who was standing by the fireplace glaring at me.

'I can't eat the food she gives us,' I replied blandly.

'Little devils, they're too fussy by half,' said the woman, continuing to look daggers at me.

'Now, now,' soothed the Welfare Officer glancing up at Mrs What-ever-her-name-was. 'I should like to speak to

Frank privately.' Well I never, someone had called me by my Christian name! The woman reluctantly headed for the door and went out, but stood on the other side of it with her ear glued to the keyhole, I'll warrant.

'Sit down Frank,' smiled the Welfare Officer. I perched myself on the edge of a kitchen chair facing him. 'Now then, we don't seem to be getting off on the right foot at all do we?' he continued in a level tone.

'I just don't like it here,' I replied.

'Well nowhere is perfect this side of Heaven,' he smiled.

'You can say that again,' I laughed.

'Listen, how would you like it if I found you somewhere else to live, Frank?' he asked. What on earth was this bloke up to? If he called me 'Frank' once more I'd faint clean away.

'It just so happens,' he continued, 'that there is a room vacant in a lady's house near Enfield. Of course it will be farther away from your place of work, but if you get up a little earlier in the morning it shouldn't make all that much difference.'

Without giving the slightest thought to the inconveniences of having to travel several miles to work, I enthusiastically agreed to the move and the following Friday evening he called to take me there. I was already packed and waiting impatiently for his arrival. I wanted to get out of the house without saying good-bye to the woman, but the Welfare Officer would not hear of it (no doubt he had to keep in with her, for there were few enough people who would take Barnardo Boys into their homes). Grudgingly I offered her my hand and insincerely thanked her for having me in the house. We then set off in the Welfare Officer's car for the new digs.

The house was spotlessly clean and my new landlady, a kindly woman in her late thirties or early forties, greeted me warmly as I entered the front door. She was a divorced woman and shared the house with her brother and his wife. I was the first boy that she had taken in and I sensed immediately that she had no ulterior motives. It was an act of pure philanthropy. She showed me the neat box-room where I was to sleep; it had been newly decorated and a brightly coloured coverlet draped the bed. It was a far cry from the reeking slum that I had just left.

When the Welfare Officer had departed, the lady took me into the kitchen and put a huge and delicious supper in front of me. The brother and his wife came into the room to meet me as I ate; they too made me feel entirely welcome. When I had consumed the last morsel of food on my plate, the lady invited me into the sitting-room and offered me a comfortable chair by the fire. I was very shy and unable to contribute very much to the conversation, but they did not force the issue in any way. I felt warm and secure in this friendly atmosphere and experienced perhaps a little of the feeling I had had when in the company of Miss Love all those years before. That night I slept peacefully in my new bed. For the first time since my discharge from Goldings I felt that there was some hope for me, in this best of all worlds.

As luck would have it the brother had a car and as he worked for a transport firm not far from the nursery, he gave me a lift to work every morning. It turned out that I did not have to get up earlier in the morning, on the contrary, I could rise half an hour later and still arrive punctually at seven.

Upon seeing the shabby state of my clothes, the landlady offered me an extended loan to buy new ones. She said that it did not matter when I paid her back, I got the impression that she would not have minded if I never did. What a contrast it all was from the behaviour that I had come to expect from people. Oddly enough I did not suspect her motives, but simply accepted her generosity with (I hope) well-mannered graciousness.

On Saturdays and Sundays the brother would take us all on drives into the country in his car. In the evenings they would treat me to a visit to the cinema and sometimes even to a light ale in the local pub. In my new suit and shoes I was no longer ashamed to be seen out and about. But how I still hated the job at the nursery. Then one Friday a blessing came to me in disguise, the foreman came around with our wage packets and with mine he handed me my Insurance Card and P45 income-tax form. I had been sacked. No reason was offered to me, and I did not ask for one. I looked upon it merely as a merciful release. I imagine the boss no longer required my services because I was idle and sullen. I had also, over the years, become a past master in the art of dumb insolence. Whatever the reason, I had been given the heave-ho and I was thoroughly delighted. In my pay packet there was a week's money and a further week's money in lieu of notice, added to this there was a couple of pounds holiday pay. Never in my life had I seen so much money all at one time, there was in the packet something over five pounds. A veritable fortune.

Though I was elated at now being free of the job, I was somewhat reluctant to tell the kind lady when I got home from work that night. I had no idea how she would take it, and I had not the slightest wish to worry or upset her. But as she would anyway find out that I had lost the job when I did not go to work on the following Monday morning, I broached the matter that evening after supper. Predictably she was very sympathetic and indeed said that I had no business in such a smelly job anyway. Her brother said that boys were always needed at his transport firm as driver's mates and that he would ask the boss if there were any vacancies the very next day. Which he duly did and I was given a start at the firm the following week. The work was far less gruelling than it had been at the nursery and far more interesting.

I was first van-boy to a funny old man with matrimonial troubles of twenty years' standing. From the time we set out in the morning till we returned to the depot in the late evening he did not stop moaning about his old woman, but his disparaging remarks about her lacked conviction, and I think that secretly he loved her dearly. Less often he talked of his only son, who had been killed in action during the war. On these rare occasions he spoke with pride and moving eloquence without any histrionics. Somewhat surprisingly he seemed to have no hate for the Germans, he maintained a dignified stiff upper lip, a well known characteristic of the British in adversity. He was Nationalistic to the roots of his being and seemed only saddened by the fact that the holocaust had cost so many young lives on both sides.

Each morning we loaded up the van with flowers from the Lea Valley and delivered them to Covent Garden Market. It was marvellous to come to London every day and I was enthralled by the hurly-burly of the market and the good-natured abuse that the porters never seemed to tire of showering on one another. It was alive and vital, I longed to be able to behave like them, and indeed tried my best to emulate them, but it was a futile attempt. My personality had been almost squashed out of existence. Since birth I had been sat on the moment I showed the slightest signs of individuality. Now that the opportunity had arrived for me to express myself freely without fear of retributive action I was totally unable to do it. There lurked just beneath the surface of my skin a sensitive artist bursting to get out, but I was thwarted at every turn by my own inadequacies. I was destined to suffer the most appalling anguish before I ultimately found the key to my life. (And still I remain my own well-seasoned worst enemy.)

Attached to the job there were many perks and a good deal of overtime, at time and a half. Some weeks I picked up as much as eight and even ten pounds in my pay-packet. I soon got the draped suit and 'creepers' I had lusted after – I looked as smart as any of the local lads when I went on the hunt for girls at the week-ends.

On Saturday afternoons the local talent, both boys and girls, congregated outside Woolworths in Waltham Cross High Street. The boys always stood apart from the girls, feigning disinterest in them, but observing them lustfully out of the corners of their eyes. The girls giggled together and talked of clothes and lipstick; though they pretended otherwise, they were well aware that they were being scrutinized like cows in a pen. Suddenly an intrepid young blood would strut over to them and invite one to the dance at the youth club that night. He would be followed by another and another, till eventually the two camps became one. Fraternization with the girls was the most popular and almost the only pastime in the town. The maids in their teens were hell-bent on getting a husband before they were twenty and the lads caddishly wanted only a 'Knee-Trembler' against the wall at the back of the youth club before the night was over. The pairing-off was a weekly ritual rhapsodically enjoyed by both sexes.

One Saturday as I lounged against a lamp-post in the High Street, wearing my powder-blue gabardine suit and crêpe shoes I saw a familiar face coming along the street towards me. It was Pedro. I knew that he was to be released from Barnardo's shortly after me, but I had not the slightest idea that he would be found a situation in the same area as me. We saw each other at precisely the same moment, and rushed to greet each other like long-lost brothers. We shook hands warmly and clapped each other on the shoulders. Pedro told me that he had only been out a couple of weeks, I knew that he could not have been discharged for much longer because he was wearing his ill-fitting deprived orphan's suit.

He had been found a job in a furniture factory near-by, and from what he told me about it he would soon be on his feet. He much admired my togs and said that he would get himself a similar outfit as soon as he had saved up enough money. That night we went to the youth club together and the following day he called at the house to meet my kind landlady.

It was nice to be with my old friend once more, for though I managed to get on with the local lads after a fashion there was not one of them whom I could call my real friend. The stigma of being a 'Banana Boy' was still upon me, I imagine.

Once more Pedro and I became inseparable. We went on the hunt for girls together, looked for fights with the local boys at the youth club together, hung about on street corners together. We were a formidable double act. Soon Pedro saved enough money to buy an outfit identical to mine in every particular, even to the colour of our socks. A boy once flirted with death by referring to us in a loud voice as the 'Dolly sisters'. We promptly took him outside and gave him the thrashing of his life.

We swaggered about the town like arrogant gangsters, indeed we emulated the bootlegging films we saw at the local fleapit until we had almost lost our own identities. We called girls 'Dolls' and boys 'Punks' and hated policemen instinctively though I have to own they never did us the slightest harm. It was a perilous course to pursue, though we were unaware of it at the time, and would not have cared if we had been. It was a fantasy to be played out to the bitter end – it lasted until I was twenty-five years old. Even during my periods of imprisonment in later life, I never let go of the romantic image that I had of gangsters. For though I broke the law incessantly I never thought of myself as a criminal (I still do not feel I have ever done a criminal act). I was just a poor fool, fighting for the right to be an individual – a freethinker – an original – an anarchist – 'Look ma I'm on top of the world,' as James Cagney said at the climax of a film entitled *White Heat* or was it *Kiss Tomorrow Goodbye*? Anything but face the facts of my life.

Just when I thought that everything was going along swimmingly, the Governor of the transport firm took me off the Covent Garden run, and put me to work with the mechanic. For some weeks I spent my days lying on my back under lorries, armed with a monkey wrench and a grease gun. During my lunch-hour the mechanic gave me driving lessons in the yard. I enjoyed being allowed behind the wheel very much, but I was far from happy wielding spanners and getting drenched with sump oil all day long. I began taking days off, feigning illness. Before long the boss wearied of my inane excuses and gave me my cards.

For a time after that I joined the ranks of the unemployed, signing on at the labour exchange twice a week and collecting a pittance in dole money on Fridays. It was during this period that I discovered that I had an almost unbelievable aptitude for listless inactivity. I could without the slightest difficulty sleep the clock round, indeed very often I would not rise from my bed till the rest of the household returned from work in the evening. These dreamy days were given up to salacious thought accompanied by much masturbation beneath the sheets. I would emerge from my room for the evening meal bleary-eyed and exhausted.

Though I was now behind with the rent my kindly landlady made little complaint at my disinterest in finding another job. But one night her brother kicked up a hell of a fuss at my ineptitude and said that I would have to clear out if I did not pull my socks up. Not wanting to be thrown out of the house, I reluctantly took a job in a tin box factory as a 'Perforator Of Talcum Powder Tops Hand Press Operator'. Well someone has to put them there, those little holes don't get there by themselves. It is the most tedious work it has ever been my misfortune to be faced with, sewing mailbags excepted.

Down the centre of the factory floor there were about twenty talcum-powder-top perforating machines, behind each sat a man on a stool, his hand on the weighted swivel handle. To one side of each man there was a huge tea-chest full of unperforated talcum-powder-tops and to the other a second tea-chest in which to deposit the talcum-powder-tops once they had been perforated. It was work that could have been done by a child of five with Herculean muscles in his right arm – strength was needed but no brain power. The perforating operation was executed as follows: take unperforated top from box, place on press, pull weighted swivel handle towards operator, let go handle which automatically returns to neutral position, take now perforated talcum top from press, place in second tea-chest. Repeat operation *ad infinitum*. A proficient operator was able to perforate about twenty-five tops per minute, though at this speed care had to be taken not to inadvertently perforate the back of the hand. Though I became quite fast I never reached Olympic standard. My mind was far too preoccupied with thoughts of the exotic bathrooms that my finished products would grace, and of the beautiful women who would sprinkle their nude bodies with its sweet-smelling contents. Sometimes I would mentally name the girl whom I would most like to have each of my completed tops. It passed the time and seemed to fit into the rhythm of the work. Christian name (put the top on the press) Surname (pull the handle, let it go and dispose of finished product). Jane Russell, Rita Hayworth, Dorothy Lamour, Jan Sterling, Veronica Lake, Betty Grable, Anna Stern, Ginger Rogers, Katharine Hepburn, Margaret Lockwood, Madeleine Carroll and always Loretta Young – for her I would have liked to have been working in a soap factory. Or better still been a sponge diver in the South Seas.

Pedro, being beautiful in all things, had now got himself a steady girl friend. She was what is known as a 'nice girl', which meant in plain language that she did not drop her drawers at the slightest provocation. She lived with her mum and dad; Pedro seemed to spend the best part of his life going around to their house, to show his honourable intentions and getting filled to capacity with home cooking. The girl's name was Violet, she hated me with a profound loathing, for no particular reason other than that she thought I was a bad influence on Pedro. The vehemence in her eyes on the now rare occasions that he and I went out on the town by ourselves (leaving her at home to wash her hair or rinse her smalls) was indeed a frightening sight to see. It looked to me as though they would soon be heading for the altar; it was a possibility too noxious for me to contemplate, so I dismissed the thought as soon as it entered my head.

Though I cannot say that I was desolated by Violet's dislike of me, I did not enjoy it overmuch, so I made myself scarce whenever she was around. It was the beginning of my isolation from the human race. I mooned around the town companionless, hating myself for my loneliness ten times a day, but treating with contempt those who would be my friends. 'Hell,' as a great thinker once wrote , 'is other people.' What cardinal sins I have been guilty of: guilt, fear, hate, remorse and the father of them all, self pity! And yet all of these defects together have given me the strength of will to be the inadequate artist I am today. The sombre truths of my existence I have, due to whatever power of concentration I have left, turned to some profit. If not for the world then at least for myself.

If by some incredible freak of circumstance writing

these painful pages should dissuade some wayward mother from abandoning her child then my polemic will not have been in vain. (The previous three and a half lines should be read to the accompaniment of Chopin's *Nocturne* in E flat major.)

I became a cinema addict, I went as often as my now meagre earnings would allow. Far and wide I would travel by bus to see pictures that I had not seen, very often I would see two shows in one day, or even sit through the same one twice. My skin was hardly exposed to the sunlight, and took on an extremely unhealthy-looking pallor. For if I wasn't working at the factory I was either in bed or huddled in the shilling stalls.

One day as I sat watching a film entitled *Blood and Sand*, starring Tyrone Power, a girl sat down next to me. So enthralled was I by what was going on on the screen (it was, I remember, the life story of a matador who having once been the darling of the crowd had now fallen from grace, but I quite forget what happened in the end) I hardly noticed her presence until suddenly as I lit my umpteenth cigarette she asked me if I would sell her one. Rather nonplussed by this unusual request I offered her one together with a lighted match, but would not accept her proffered three-halfpence. Thanking me profusely she put the cigarette between her lips and I set light to it with the spluttering match. We then fell silent, but were now acutely aware of each other's presence as we sat with our eyes riveted to the screen. My throat dry and my heart pounding, I moved my foot into the darkened area of floor beneath her seat, without warning she too moved her leg towards mine – it was as though there was mental telepathy between us. Our limbs touched and an electric charge galvanized my body; neither of us moved a muscle. We just sat there staring at the screen, but I think neither of us were now much interested in the film, certainly I was not. At an agonizingly slow speed I inched my right arm around her waist, she made no attempt to stop me. Mustering all my courage I placed my left hand on her knee, hardly daring to breathe I gently began to stroke the inside of her thigh. Her hand came down on top of mine and she turned her face towards me, still we did not dare to speak. Our lips met in a rapturous kiss and my hand ventured farther up her skirt whilst with the other I caressed the taut nipples of her breasts. Still we spoke no word. My hand had now reached her crutch, for a moment I hesitated from fear, then, throwing caution to the winds, I boldly pushed aside the flimsy material. She moved slightly and forced her tongue between my teeth, while her hand went to my flies, fumbled with the buttons for a moment and was then inside. It was the most ineffable and unexpected liaison of my life. What a delicious chance meeting it was, we spent another hour fondling each other. I then whispered in her ear that I would like to go and invited her to come with me. Still not having uttered a word she got to her feet and followed me out of the cinema. What a shock I got when I saw her in daylight, she was without doubt the ugliest girl I had ever seen in my life (though I dare say I have seen worse since). She had a bumpy figure and a really awful face from which bulging cod-like eyes protruded. I had thought that I would take her for some tea, then find a secluded spot in which to tail her. But fear of being seen in the town with such a frightful-looking girl ungallantly overcame me. Hastily saying that I had to go to the Gents, which indeed I had, I asked her to wait for me in the foyer of the cinema. Craftily I sneaked out of another exit and leapt on the first bus that passed by. I never saw the unfortunate girl again and never since have I spent such an enjoyable afternoon in the cinema.

. . . . .

In the sitting-room of the house where I lived there was a cocktail cabinet, which seemed to be always well stocked with booze. In the evenings the family would pour themselves drinks, but only on special occasions would they offer me one, thinking perhaps that I was still too young for hard liquor. However when I was alone in the house I would without the slightest hesitation help myself to a snifter and more often than not more than one.

I began to get quite a taste for the stuff. One day I sneaked a couple of small glasses of sherry and then a third. I had got the taste for it. Not caring if I was caught I took the bottle from the cabinet and proceeded to polish off three parts of it; before long I was dead drunk. Later the brother's wife returned to the house and was greatly shocked to see the condition I was in. It had taken me badly and I was in belligerent mood. She asked me why I had done such a stupid thing, I told her to get stuffed. She told me not to talk to her like that. I told her I would talk to her how I liked. She said she would report me. I told her to get stuffed again. And so the inane wrangle went on, she saying one thing and I another, till in the end I lost my temper and abused her mercilessly calling her a stupid old cow. Terrified by this she ran from the room and got a carving knife from the kitchen, thinking that at any moment I was going to commit physical violence on her. Waving the knife under my nose, she hysterically told me to get out of the house and not return till I was sober. Unnerved by the imminent dangers of staying I rushed from the house, before it was too late. On a grass verge not far off, I lay on the ground and fell into a drunken stupor, from which I awoke several hours later with a monumental hangover (the predecessor of a thousand I have had since).

Nervously I made my way home once more, fearful of the consequences that awaited me. Sneaking in the back door I tried to get up to my room unnoticed by the family, whose voices I could hear in the living-room. As I approached the foot of the stairs the door opened and the landlady came out.

'Ah there you are,' she said in a friendly tone. 'Come in, I want to have a word with you.' She stood aside and I forlornly walked past her into the room, my head bowed in shame. The brother's wife glanced up at me from a chair by the fire, and, to my utter amazement, smiled.

'I hear you got quite a skinful,' said the brother who was standing by the window.

'I'm sorry,' I mumbled.

'Would you like a cup of tea?' asked the landlady who had followed me into the room. I nodded yes.

'Don't look so miserable, and sit down,' said the wife. I slumped into a chair. 'I hope you have learned your lesson,' she continued good-humouredly.

The extraordinary thing was they were forgiving me for my bad behaviour without demanding retribution, a situation I was by no means used to. When I had drunk the tea I cheered up a little and apologized more profusely, though it was not demanded of me. Incredible are the ways of people; I have for lesser offences been severely punished. Not being able to leave well enough alone, I offered to buy a bottle of sherry to replace the one that I had drunk. But they would not hear of it, I was only asked never to do such a stupid thing again. I was beginning to realize that not all people were bad. To make up for my misbehaviour I bought the wife a huge bunch of flowers, the following pay day. Thus the matter was closed.

When Pedro could escape the clutches of Violet we still went out together, and had of late taken to going farther afield. The world, we were slowly discovering, was wider than Waltham Cross. From the trolley bus terminal, transport could be got to places as far away as Ponders End, Dalston,

Stoke Newington and even Tottenham Court Road in the heart of London. I greatly enjoyed these excursions and was much enamoured by the bright lights of the West End. On one of these trips I paid my first visit to Soho – though I did not know it at the time. Little did I realize that within a year or two it would become my place. The place that I still visit with monotonous regularity.

In Dalston there was a tattoo artist whose emporium was greatly patronized by the local lads, arm decorations being very popular at the time. One Saturday afternoon Pedro and I visited the place and rather stupidly had a woman put on our right forearms. We both chose the same one, a rather nationalistic looking lady carrying a sword (supposedly to protect her honour) and wearing high boots, a flowing cape and trapeze-artiste leotard. The whole thing was done in blue and red indelible ink. How proud of ourselves we were when we emerged from the shop, having braved unflinchingly the agonies of the tattoo-artist's electric needle. Ostentatiously we rolled up our sleeves and paraded around the town showing our newly acquired ornamentations, almost as though they were medals awarded for bravery. I thought my tattoo made me look tough and sexy; compounding the folly I visited the emporium several weeks later and had an anchor, incorporating anchor-chain, sailor's head and distant sunset, engraved for life upon my left arm.

To jaunty effect we at different times took to smoking pipes and wearing stetson hats. How the girls did ogle us as we swept by with haughty indifference. I found that by ignoring girls I had far more success with them than I had when I sniffed around them like a dog. Girls adored to be taken by force, by coarse young ruffians out for a lark. But all the girls who fell for me were onto a good hiding to nothing, for if they would not let me *do* them the first night I took them out I never saw them again. Conversely if they did I lost respect for them and would see them no more. Such are the ways of randy boys since time began.

But it just isn't possible to win them all, for one day I found myself seriously stuck on a girl named Edith; she was sixteen years old, and had dark hair and a sad expression that seemed to darken her eyes perpetually. She worked behind the household goods counter in Woolworth's. God help me, I was now in the same ridiculous position as Pedro. As a matter of fact Edith and Violet got on like a house on fire. And Violet somewhat alarmingly became far more friendly towards me now that it looked as though I was settling down with a steady girl friend. So the four of us now started going out together, to the pictures twice a week and the youth club three times a week and the dance-hall once, the other night we didn't see them – hair-washing, etc.

I took Edith around to my lodgings one night and introduced her to my landlady. I had hoped that it was one of the nights that the family would go out, in which case I would lumber Edith up to my bedroom, but it wasn't, so I did not get the chance. I do not think my landlady was over-impressed by her, a fact that did not over-surprise me. For certainly Edith was greatly lacking in brains and her conversation was more often than not putrid. But there was something about her that fascinated me, though I now quite forget what it was.

One day I got home from work and noticed that a great change had come over my landlady. As I came into the house through the kitchen door, she was at the stove cooking the evening meal. I greeted her cheerily but she made no reply. Thinking that perhaps she had not heard me I repeated my greeting, glancing in my direction she glowered, then without uttering a word turned her back on me and left the room. What on earth had I done? Going into the bathroom I took off my overalls and washed, then went downstairs once more.

The brother and his wife were dining out that night, we were therefore alone in the house. I sat down at the kitchen table and waited for the supper to be served up, I tried to make some conversation with the back of my landlady's head as she banged the pots about on the stove in an agitated fashion but she completely ignored me. I was absolutely mystified by her behaviour and though I racked my brain could not find a reason for it. Still remaining silent she banged a plate of food down in front of me and left the room. It was the first time since I had lived there that she had not sat down at the table and eaten with me. Moodily, I ate the meal then went into the sitting-room; she glanced up at me as I entered the room, glowered, then went back to darning a pair of socks she had in her hand.

'Is there anything wrong?' I asked mildly.

'You may well ask,' she snapped.

'Pardon?'

'It won't do you any good looking so innocent.'

'I haven't done nothing.'

'Haven't you just!'

My confusion mounted, with a shrug of my shoulders I sat in the other arm-chair and picked up the daily paper.

'You're a dirty beast,' she exploded angrily as I buried my nose into the centre pages. Lowering the paper I glanced up at her inquiringly.

'I suppose you think I don't know what that is all over your sheets?' she asked, glaring straight into my eyes for the first time. For a moment I had no idea what she was talking about.

'I've been married you know.' The tone of this inept remark seemed to indicate that it had great significance. The truth of what she was alluding to suddenly hit me like a bolt from the blue. As the realization crept over me, the hairs at the nape of my neck began to prickle and the blood pulsated to my cheeks, turning them pink. So that was it, she had found the telltale spunk-stains on my bed linen. A testimony to my nightly lascivious indecencies. I might have known sooner, for that was the weekly sheet-changing day. I was struck dumb from embarrassment. What could I say anyway? Excuses cannot be made for nature. I felt filthy to the core of my being. Not because of what I had done, but because I had been caught out.

'I have never known anything so *dirty*,' she said in disgust. 'I don't want you in my house any longer. I have already written to Barnardo's and told them to take you away.'

'Oh please,' I pleaded, now close to tears. 'Please don't tell them.' But it was a futile plea.

'It's too late, I already have.'

'But I can't help it, honestly I can't.'

'I will not have such vile practices going on in my house,' she said adamantly; with that she rose to her feet and stalked out of the room. The very sight of me now disgusted her. Thoroughly dejected I went up to my room and jerked myself senseless.

(How great is the flood of life-giving semen wasted by British youth. All do it but none will admit it and to be caught at it is a carnal sin so impure that the proud cock-jerking youth may never again lift his head in respectable circles. Damnation to purity!)

The following morning I rose early and crept out of the house before breakfast, unnoticed. I had donned my best suit, for I had not the slightest intention of going to work that day. As I roamed around the town, my eyes cast to the ground whenever a fellow pedestrian passed by, I felt now that the whole world must know my guilty secret. It happened that a fair had come to town, and was rapidly being erected by an army of tough-looking young men, on the outskirts of the town. For a time I sat on a grass bank watching them work, like ants; each seemed instinctively to know his job as they scurried about, lifting heavy pieces of scaffolding and steel plates. How happy they seemed in their work, singing and making jokes as they toiled. Their high spirits did much to elevate my acute depression. I was enthralled by the colour and blatant vitality of the scene and heartily wished that I could be part of it. But what would they want with the likes of me, a weak-looking boy fallen from grace?

In the middle of the morning the men knocked off work for an hour and repaired to a café near-by for food. Somewhat hesitantly I followed behind and entering the café sat down at a table not far from them; they were boisterously good humoured and molested the poor waitress till the proprietor was compelled to intervene. It looked as though at any minute they would strip the clothes off her.

'Give us egg and chips and getcha knickers down darlin'!' roared a huge young man in his early twenties with greasy black hair, taking a swipe at the girl's behind. His companion roared with laughter and the proprietor threatened to throw them out if they did not behave.

'Leave orf Guv,' laughed one of the men. 'We're only 'avin' a bit of a giggle ain't we.'

'Just keep your voices down,' said the proprietor and stalked off. But they were only subdued momentarily, for no sooner had the owner departed than they started up again chi-iking each other bawdily, their dialogue liberally peppered with four-letter swear words. Several middle-aged workmen eyed them distastefully but none dared to complain, wisely fearing a swift punch on the nose, no doubt. Suddenly at a particularly scurrilous remark about the waitress's bottom I too burst into laughter. The men glanced in my direction, one of them winked at me, then continued with the bacchanalian revelry. But the ice had been broken, they had noticed me. When they had finished eating they gathered around a pin-table machine standing in the corner of the room, one after the other banging pennies into the slot and smashing the balls around the light-flashing, bell-ringing table, scoring phenomenally at times amid cheers, but more often than not tilting the machine amid foul abuse. When at last they left I trailed behind them, hoping against hope that one of them would speak to me, but none did.

Once more I sat on the grass and watched them work (watching others toil being a favourite pastime of the British). Then mustering up my courage I sauntered over to the machine they were building and somewhat hesitantly chatted them up.

'Wotcha kid, you come from rahnd 'ere?' asked the big bloke with the greasy black hair.

'Sort of,' I replied.

'Wotcha mean?'

'Well I live around here but I don't really come from here.'

'Is that so,' he said, passing off my confusing remark.

'Where did the fair come from before here?' I asked leaping out of the way of four men bearing down on me with a huge steel plate on their shoulders.

'All over,' said the man, levering the plate into position when the men had dumped it on the ground.

'What do you think the chances are of my getting a job?' I asked, coming straight to the point.

'Pretty good, I reckon,' smiled the man, exposing dirty teeth. 'See that wagon over there?' he went on, pointing to a caravan some way off. 'Well, go over there and ask for the Guv'ner, 'is name's 'Arry Burns. Nah I can't stand 'ere rabbitin' t' yer no more. We gotta get this bastard up before it pisses darn wiv rain.'

'Okay,' I said, 'thanks a lot.'

The caravan door was opened to me by a middle-aged woman. 'May I speak to Mr Burns?'

"Arry there's a boy out 'ere wants t' see ya!' she yelled over her shoulder.

"Ang on a minute,' said a gruff voice. Mr Burns appeared in the doorway after a short pause and peered down at me. He was a stocky little man, wearing a black bowler and several days growth of beard.

'Wotcha want son?' he asked good-naturedly.

'Well, I was wondering if you would give me a job,' I replied fearfully.

'You ever work on a gaff before?' he asked. (Gaff is the original 'travellers'' name for a fair, now much abused by cockneys, who use it to describe any confined space.)

'No sir,' I replied. 'But I am willing to learn.'

'Well I dunno, if ya ain't got no experience.'

'I'll do anything sir, please give me a try at least,' I pleaded. For a few moments he studied me in silence, then smiling broadly asked. 'You on the run from the law, are ya?'

'No sir,' I replied in alarm.

'Okay, I'll take ya word for it, fahsands wouldn't,' he laughed. 'Go over there t' the dodgems and arst Blacky t' give ya a start. Fiver a week an' ya kip, all right?

'Yes sir,' I exclaimed somewhat over-enthusiastically.

'You gotcha cards?' he asked as I was about to run off.

'Well, they're at the firm I've been working for but I can get them,' I said

'See ya do, all I'm short of is bovva wiv the law. 'Ow old are ya any'ow?'

'Eighteen sir,' I said, adding a couple of years to my life. Before he could question me further I ran off in the direction of the dodgems and asked for Blacky, who turned out to be the one with the greasy black hair and muscles.

'First off yer'll 'ave ter getcha self some old clobber,' when I told him that Mr Burns had given me a

[158]

'I've got some at home,' I said.

'Well don't just stand there go 'ome and get 'em.'

'Okay,' I replied and was off like a shot.

'Come back at six in time for when we open,' he shouted after me.

It was still early afternoon. I knew that if I hurried I could get into the house, collect my things and get out again before the rest of the household got home from work. Running as hard as my legs would carry me I reached the house in double-quick time, rushed up to my room, threw my belongings into my suitcase and tore out again. Not a moment did I pause, for time I felt was of the essence. With the prospect of the new and exciting life before me, the degradation I had felt earlier in the day had subsided. Even so I was too pusillanimous ever to face my hitherto kindly landlady again. I must run and hide – I have been running ever since from one thing and another, and am now an adept escapologist.

Having got clear of the house, I breathed a sigh of relief, got a bus to the Tin Box factory where I demanded my cards, which the management were delighted to give me without question.

Then back to the fairground I went, eager to begin work as a 'Dodgem Greaser'. The heavy work had now been completed, the cars were on the track pushed to one end, ready for the first customers.

'Wotcha kid,' said Blacky as I approached carrying my suitcase. 'Dump ya gear in that wagon over there then come and give us a 'and t' put in the light bulbs.' I rushed off in the direction he had indicated and climbed the steps into the brightly painted wagon. The inside was dank and musty; along each side there were three-tier bunks – about a dozen in all. Quickly I changed into my working clothes and bolted back to the dodgem track.

'You start that side, an' I'll start the uvva,' said Blacky, handing me a huge basket of coloured electric light bulbs.

Clearly I remember how keen and over-excited I was as I commenced to carry out this simple task. These were the most alive people that I had ever met in my life, a motley crew of nomadic people: didikois, travellers, deserters from the Forces, deserters from life. A sprinkling of gipsies with noble Romany blood in their veins, their horse-drawn wagons brightly coloured in every conceivable hue, burnished copper pots and pans hanging from the sides glinting in the sun. I romantically thought how marvellous it would be to marry a wild gipsy beauty and just roam about the country making pegs and eating hedgehogs.

I promised myself that I would visit the caravan of 'THE ONE AND ONLY GYPSY ROSE LEE' (one of a dozen fortune-tellers boasting the title up and down the country) and get her to tell me what life had in store for me, but I never did. Which is just as well, I suppose.

At six in the evening the mighty electricity generators were switched on and the whole fairground came alive with coloured lights and blaring music. The people from the town began to arrive, slowly at first then in droves till by eight o'clock the world and his wife were there, riding the machines, trying their luck on the hoopla, getting the life frightened out of them on the ghost train. The boxing-booth barker challenged the local lads to face his battered pugs: 'A fiver if you can go three rounds with Mighty Mike MacCraw.'

'Roll up roll up, see the beautiful maiden from the exotic Orient dance the dance of the seven veils,' bellowed the man wearing a loud suit and straw hat at the side-show next door. 'Rescued from the harem of the sheik of Arabee. She dances naked before your very eyes.' The men flocked inside, watched by the narrow-minded ladies from the local Moral Welfare Society.

'Roll up for the coco-nut shy!'
'Round she goes where she stops nobody knows.'
'Get your candy floss here.'
'Buy a sprig of lucky heather for the lady sir.'
'Shilling a ride half-price for the kiddies.'
'Come and see the bearded lady. The goat with two heads. The reptile girl, the only one in captivity. Don't be afraid lady she won't bite you we only fed her last week.' All was a hurly-burly of life and activity. My eyes wide with wonder I surveyed the scene absorbing every minute detail, missing nothing. Never before in my life had I seen such a wondrous sight. And to think that I was part of it!

Blacky instructed me to collect the fares from drivers who got into the cars numbered one to five. It was liable to be rather hazardous leaping from one car to the next, as they whizzed around the track crashing into each other. I had to hang on with one hand and collect money from the passengers with the other. But it was a great lark and I soon became as nimble on my feet as the best of them. Suddenly I jumped onto the back of a car and found myself looking into Pedro's smiling face, he was sitting in the car with Violet beside him. So astonished was I by his sudden appearance that I almost lost my balance and fell under the wheels of the car behind.

'What are you doing here?' exclaimed Pedro.

'Can't talk now,' I replied grabbing his shilling and leaping to the next car. When the ride had come to an end, he approached me as I leaned against the side rail waiting for the cars to fill up again. I told him that I had got a job on the fair, and asked him why he should not join me. 'After all it is a way of seeing the country and getting paid for it,' I said. This remark, as may well be imagined, went down like a lead balloon with Violet, who stood silently fuming as I spoke excitedly on the eventful life I now foresaw for myself. 'Well you might have told Edith,' she snapped as I turned from them to do more work. 'We waited for you for an hour. In the end she said that she didn't want to go to the fair by herself.' I had not given a thought to my steady girl friend who in any event did not fit into my new plans. Even if I had not been going away, she would have packed me in of her own volition as soon as she heard of my sporting affairs from my landlady, who would be bound to make inquiries (and tell all) when she discovered that I had gone missing. I was too embarrassed to tell Pedro the real reason why I was running away in front of Violet. If we had been alone I would have told him right enough, even boastfully and we would have had a good laugh about it. But provincial girls can be very shocked by such things despite the fact that masturbation is by no means a practice confined to the male sex.

I told Pedro that I would come to see him as soon as I got some time off. I then jumped onto the back of a passing dodgem car and careered off around the track.

At half-past eleven the fair closed down for the night, I was absolutely exhausted by the sustained agility that I had somehow kept up for more than five hours. Every muscle in my body ached, many of which I had not been aware existed before. But Mr Burns said that I had done well, and Blacky clapped me on the shoulder and said: 'Not bad for ya first night, kid, yer'll soon get the 'ang of it.' Praise indeed. We then went to the café and ate meat pies and mashed potatoes. The wagon where I was to sleep was unsanitary and freezing cold. On the bunk was a filthy palliasse filled with mouldering straw and the bedcovers were nothing more than old sacks. Never before had I been so uncomfortably housed, but the excitement of the great adventure that I was embarking upon more than compensated for the hardship I had to endure. (In later life I was destined to endure far worse.)

During those first few days Blacky was a tower of strength to me. The work was gruelling and by the end of the first week I thought that I should never survive it. But my new-found friend helped me whenever he could by taking over my share of the work when the Governor was not about. He also taught me to palm the customers' change, by counting it from the right hand into the left; but secreting half a crown or more between the forefinger and third when handing over the money. So intent were the gullible public upon the joy-ride that not one of them tumbled to the fiddle.

By the end of the second week I had become fairly used to the work and unsanitary way of life. Though washing was difficult I somehow managed to keep clean. On the Sunday, after a stand-up bath in cold water at the back of the wagon, I set out for my last meeting with Pedro. We met outside the cinema and went for a walk around the town; he had managed to get out of meeting Violet under some pretext, and I had not the slightest wish to bid farewell to Edith. For a time we ambled along in silence, neither of us knowing quite what to say to the other.

'Why don't you come with me?' I asked on impulse.

'It's not for me,' smiled Pedro. 'I've got a good job with prospects. I guess it's worth sticking at it for a while.' Barnardo's indoctrination had worked on him, if not on me. It looked very much as though he was going to be a solid citizen, I saw no point in attempting to persuade him further so we talked of other things. The afternoon wore on in an atmosphere of gloom, and I think by early evening we both felt that the parting was being laboured. Nevertheless we went together to the youth club and spent a couple of hours playing ping-pong and darts. At about nine he walked me back to the fairground and we parted company after a ludicrously solemn handshake. For a few minutes I stood by the steps of the wagon and watched him go; tears came to my eyes as I turned away. I never saw Pedro again from that day to this. I sometimes wonder what happened to him, but not often. I imagine he is now one of the last master craftsmen in the country, married to Violet and has a brood of kids, perhaps.

The following morning we 'pulled down' the machine and left the town in convoy with all the other people who went to make up the fair. And I left with it, in the cab of a four-wheel-drive articulated lorry drawing three trailers.

I had enrolled in the university of life. One summer's day a decade later, I bought a sixpenny exercise-book and a pencil, went into Hyde Park, sat on a bench and began to write.

## HOGARTH FICTION

*All in a Lifetime* by Walter Allen
New Introduction by Alan Sillitoe

*Epitaph of a Small Winner* by Machado de Assis
Translated and Introduced by William L. Grossman

*Ballantyne's Folly* by Claud Cockburn
New Introduction by Andrew Cockburn

*Such is Life* by Tom Collins
New Introduction by David Malouf

*Chance* by Joseph Conrad
New Introduction by Jane Miller

*Born in Exile* by George Gissing
New Introduction by Gillian Tindall
*The Emancipated* by George Gissing
New Introduction by John Halperin
*The Whirlpool* by George Gissing
New Introduction by Gillian Tindall
*Will Warburton* by George Gissing
New Introduction by John Halperin

*Saturday Night at the Greyhound* by John Hampson
New Introduction by Christopher Hawtree

*Her Privates We* by Frederic Manning
New Introduction by Lyn Macdonald

*Catharine Furze* by Mark Rutherford
*Clara Hopgood* by Mark Rutherford
*The Revolution in Tanner's Lane* by Mark Rutherford
New Afterwords by Claire Tomalin

*The Last Man* by Mary Shelley
New Introduction by Brian Aldiss

*The Smith of Smiths* by Hesketh Pearson
New Introduction by Richard Ingrams

*Flannelled Fool* by T.C. Worsley
New Introduction by Alan Ross

# Frank Norman
## *Bang to Rights*

New Introduction by Jeffrey Bernard

'A natural comic writer' – *V. S. Pritchett*

'A potentially dangerous man' – *Raymond Chandler*
(from his Preface)

During the Fifties' assault on The Establishment, Frank Norman found himself catapulted from the wide-boy streets of Soho to national notoriety with *Bang to Rights*, his headlong account of three years in the nick. One of the first documentaries of a gaol-bird's life, complete with slang, feuds and spells in chokey, it is as pacey and hilarious as its celebrated descendants, like television's *Minder* or *Porridge*. It is also a memorable and bitter protest against the brutality of imprisonment.

# Richard Cobb
## *Still Life*
### Sketches from a Tunbridge Wells Childhood

*Still Life* is a classic memoir. In it, Richard Cobb takes us through the streets and houses of his childhood – down Poona Road, along by the Grove Bowling Club, and on past the taxidermist's and 'Love, Fruit and Vegetables' shop – recapturing, with the innocence of a lonely boy, the snobberies and eccentricities of secure middle-class England in the Twenties and Thirties.

'strange and wonderful' – Hilary Spurling, *Observer*

'a rare treasure' – John Carey, *The Sunday Times*